turkish phrase book

turkish phrase book

Yusuf Mardin

Routledge
London

*First published in 1970
Reprinted 1974
Revised edition 1984
Reprinted 1988 by*

*Routledge
11 New Fetter Lane, London EC4P 4EE
29 West 35th Street, New York NY 10001*

© Yusuf Mardin 1970, 1984

*Printed and bound in Great Britain by
Cox & Wyman Ltd, Reading*

*All rights reserved. No part of this book may be
reprinted or reproduced or utilized in any form or
by any electronic, mechanical, or other means, now
known or hereafter invented, including photocopying
and recording, or in any information storage or
retrieval system, without permission in writing
from the publishers.*

ISBN 0 415 02767 5

To the memory of
my mother

Bedriye Mardin

who inspired in me
a wanderlust

Contents

1 The language in general 1
The Turkish alphabet 1
Vowel harmony 2
Gender 3
Article 3
The plural suffix 3
Short note on pronunciation 3
Stress 4
Word order 5
Assimilation 5

2 Some essentials of Turkish grammar 6
Nouns 6
Declension of nouns 6
Varieties of suffixes 7
Possessive suffixes 8
Personal pronouns 8
Adjectives 9
Adverbs 9
Post-positions 10
Conjunctions 10
Interjections 10
The verb 10
Forms of the verb 13

3 Useful expressions 14
Important phrases 14
Greetings and leave-takings 16
Thanks 16
Requests 17
Regrets 17
Wishes 18
Enquiries and difficulties 18

Contents

Useful expressions (*continued*) Notices 20
　　　　　　　　　　　　　　　　Regulatory signs 21
　　　　　　　　　　　　　　　　Traffic signs 22

4 Money 24　　　　　　　　　　Numbers 26
　　　　　　　　　　　　　　　　Conversion tables 29
　　　　　　　　　　　　　　　　　Distance 29
　　　　　　　　　　　　　　　　　Length 30
　　　　　　　　　　　　　　　　　Altitude 30
　　　　　　　　　　　　　　　　　Weight 31
　　　　　　　　　　　　　　　　　Pressure 31
　　　　　　　　　　　　　　　　　Temperature 31
　　　　　　　　　　　　　　　　　Clothing sizes 32
　　　　　　　　　　　　　　　　　Tipping 33
　　　　　　　　　　　　　　　　　Conversion table 33

5 Time 34　　　　　　　　　　　Days of the week 35
　　　　　　　　　　　　　　　　Time expressions 35
　　　　　　　　　　　　　　　　Months and seasons 36
　　　　　　　　　　　　　　　　Telling the time 37

6 Weather and geographical expressions 40

7 Countries; nationalities; family and relationships 44

8 Travel 49　　　　　　　　　　Air travel 49
　　　　　　　　　　　　　　　　Travel by rail 53
　　　　　　　　　　　　　　　　Cruising and Yachting 58
　　　　　　　　　　　　　　　　Coach travel and the 'Dolmuş' 64

9 Motoring 68　　　　　　　　　Complaints at service stations 71
　　　　　　　　　　　　　　　　Requests at garages 72
　　　　　　　　　　　　　　　　Questions and directions 73

10 Camping, caravanning and cycling 75　　Camping 75
　　　　　　　　　　　　　　　　Caravanning 76
　　　　　　　　　　　　　　　　Cycling 78

Contents

11 Hotels 82

General 82
Overnight stay 89
Post 89
Laundry and cleaning 90

12 Meals and restaurants 91

Food in general 91
Turkish national dishes 91
Drinks 92
Ways of cooking 95
On the menu 95
Kinds of cheese 97
Kinds of bread 97
Kinds of sea-food 97
Poultry and game 97
Kinds of meat 98
Some sweets and desserts 98

13 Shopping 102

A list of shopkeepers 102
Useful words 103
Colours 105
Post office and telephone 109
Chemist, barber and hairdresser 112
Photography 116

14 Paying a visit and writing a letter 119

Paying a visit 120
Writing a letter 121
  A business letter 123
  An application for a licence 123
  An informal letter of invitation 124
  An acceptance 124
  Regrets 125
  A letter of thanks 125

15 Recreation 126

Sports 126
Games 127
Entertainments 128

16 Sightseeing 131

Visiting Turkish baths 132

17 Animals and vegetations 136   Animals 137
Vegetation 138

18 Hunting and fishing 140

19 Accident and loss of property 143

20 Visiting the doctor 147   Illness 147
Parts of the body 148
Questions asked by the doctor 149
Complaints of the patient 150
At the doctor's 151
At the dentist's 152

21 Calendar of Events in Turkey 154

1 The language in general

The Turkish Alphabet

Letters	Name	Pronunciation
A a	a	sun, cut, come
B b	be	bed, buy, bill
C c	ce	jar, jelly, jam
Ç ç	çe	church, chapel, child
D d	de	dear, doll, did
E e	e	red, bed, net
F f	fe	fine, fair, foul
G g	ge	gale, good, guy
Ğ ğ	yumuşak ge	(prolongs the preceding vowel) weight, neighbour
H h	he	hard, hill, hell
İ i	i	sit, thin, pin
I ı	ı	Cyril, wanted, syllable
J j	je	pleasure, measure, French (juste, jeune)
K k	ke, ka	kite, cold, cat
L l	le	lilac, lull, lily
M m	me	me, mine, mime
N n	ne	nine, no, name
O o	o	poet, author
Ö ö	ö	French (deux, seul), German (Köln, König)
P p	pe	pebble, pie, pipe
R r	re	rhyme, red, ready
S s	se	sister, similar, send
Ş ş	şe	shoe, sharp, short
T t	te	tell, truth, time

Letters	Name	Pronunciation
U u	u	put, foot, bull
Ü ü	ü	French (tu, sur), German (Glück, über)
V v	ve	away, weight
Y y	ye	year, young, youth
Z z	ze	zebra, zero, zeal

Vowel harmony

The Turkish language is sweet and melodious, mainly due to the laws of vowel harmony, whereby words beginning with front or back vowels preserve the same quality throughout. It is spoken by more than 150 million people from Macedonia to Siberia. Turkish is an easy logical language. There is no gender, no *he*, *she* or *it*, but one word for all three. The *der*, *die*, *das* of German, the nightmare of the learner, are not found in Turkish.

There are eight vowels in the Turkish language, which are divided into two groups. The first group is (e, i, ö, ü) forming the front vowels and the second group (a, ı, o, u) forming the back vowels. In Turkish, adjectives are obtained from nouns, and from adjectives and nouns, verbs are created. The language is in conformity with the modern science of phonetics – spelling and pronunciation are regular. It is formed of sounds which are the natural result of the laws of position and inflection of the tongue, and the movements of the lips and jaws, and every word is pronounced as it is written. The only exception is the soft (g), which is written as (ğ) and serves to lengthen the sound of the vowel it follows.

The language is based on the principle of vowel harmony. In other words, if the vowel of the first syllable of a word is a front vowel, the vowels of the subsequent syllables have to be front vowels. While, if the vowel of the first syllable of a word is a back vowel, so are the vowels of subsequent syllables. Suffixes have, as a rule, two forms: one with a front vowel and used with front-vowelled words; another with a back vowel, used with back-vowelled words.

Another factor that makes Turkish a musical language is the abundance of front vowels, particularly of (ü) and (ö). Although these

The language in general

vowels may seem difficult for an English student at first, those who have studied French find them in *sur* and *tu* (ü) and in *jeu* and *deux* (ö).

The back vowel (ı) which is considered by some linguists as non-existent in English, may be found in such words as *Cyril*, *hospitable*, *remarkable*, and *wanted*. For an English speaker, the one difficulty is the pronunciation of words ending in (ir), (ır), (ür), (ur), (er), (or), and (ar). He is apt to draw the tongue backwards, instead of forwards, to a position almost touching the palate. Words ending in (r) must always be sounded.

Gender

Turkish nouns, adjectives and personal pronouns have no gender. One could use the word *erkek–male* and the word *dişi–female*, to express the sex of an animal. *Kız* or *kadın* to denote female, and *erkek* to denote male, can also be placed in front of a noun to show the sex of human beings.

Article

There is no article in Turkish. By placing the noun in the objective case, one makes definite the object represented by the noun. When the object of the verb is indefinite, it is in the nominative case, by itself or preceded by *bir* (*a*) or (*an*).

The plural suffix

The plural sign is either *ler* or *lar* to be added to nouns. *Lar* is added to the end of a word with back vowels, and *ler* to the end of a word with front vowels. Once the plural sign is added to a noun, the other suffixes follow the plural sign. The plural of the third person plural of any verb is also formed by adding *ler* or *lar* to the third person singular of that verb.

Short note on pronunciation

The Turkish alphabet is made up of eight vowels and twenty-one consonants. Most of the consonants have much the same value as in English and the vowels as in French or Italian.

While (q), (w) and (x) do not appear in the Turkish alphabet, there are six new letters, namely, (ç), (ğ), (ı), (ş), (ö) and (ü). There are also other letters which exist in the English alphabet but are pronounced differently.

(c)   pronounced like (j) in *jar, jury* and *jazz*.

(ç)   pronounced like (ch), in *church, chapel, child*.

(g)   pronounced like the hard (g) of English, as in *gale*.

(ğ)   never occurs at the beginning of a word, is silent and is used to lengthen a preceding vowel.

(h)   always pronounced, as in *hard, hill, hell*.

(ı)   undotted (i), pronounced like *Cyril, wanted*, something between (i) in *big* and (u) in *bug*. It is similar to the general obscure vowel, invariably used in the notation of (-tion), (-able) in English.

(j)   pronounced as in French *jeune, juste* or as in *pleasure* and *measure* in English.

(ö)   pronounced as in (eu) in *deux* and *seul* in French or (ö) in *König* and *Köln* in German.

(s)   always an (s) sound as in *sister* and *similar*, not sometimes (z) as in *treason* in English.

(ş)   like (sh) in *shoe, shine*.

(ü)   like the (u) in *tu, sur* in French and the (ü) in *Glück, für* in German.

(r)   always pronounced as it is by the Scots, not silent when it comes at the end of a word like *better* and *far*.

Stress

Stress is not powerful as in English, but is much more equally divided. Generally it falls on the last syllable of a word. However, in the names of places, and in adverbs, conjunctions and interjections, the stress is usually on the first syllable. In compound words, the stress falls on the last syllable of the first element. Mosquito is *sivrisinek* in Turkish, i.e., a pointed-fly, and the accent falls on *-ri*, the second syllable.

In negative statements and questions, the stress always occurs on the syllable preceding the negative or interrogative particles.

KEY TO PRONUNCIATION
c (jar), ç (church), g (gale), ğ (lengthen the preceding vowel), h (hill), ı (Cyril), j (Fr. *jeune*), ö (Fr. *peu* or Ger. *Köln*), s (sister), ş (shoe), ü (Fr. *dune* or Ger. Glück)

Word order

In a sentence the subject whether a noun or a pronoun comes at the beginning, while the verb comes at the end. However, there are certain instances when this rule is not strictly observed. When writing poetry, it is permissible to change the word order, and in conversation when one is using the imperative word for a simple request or command, the verb can be brought to the beginning of a sentence for the sake of emphasis.

In a sentence, a definite precedes an indefinite word, and qualifying words precede the words they qualify. Emphasis is obtained by placing the qualifying word nearer the word it qualifies. Expressions of time, usually come at the beginning of a sentence before or after the subject and they precede expressions of place.

Assimilation

In Turkish there are no instances of a word in which a syllable ending with a vowel is followed with another syllable beginning with a vowel. That is to say, two successive vowels, as a rule, do not appear in Turkish. When a suffix beginning with a vowel, has to be added to a word already ending in a vowel, then for the sake of the rule of vowel harmony, either one of the following letters (n) (s) (ş) or (y) is inserted. These letters are known as the letters of assimilation.

2 Some essentials of Turkish grammar

Nouns

Nouns in Turkish are divided into proper and common nouns. Common nouns are in turn divided into abstract, collective and compound nouns. Nouns are made plural by affixing (-ler) to words with front vowels, and (-lar) to words with back vowels. Unlike Latin or German, the declension of nouns in Turkish is regular and invariable. There are no first, second, third forms of declensions with different suffixes. One can only see minor changes in words due to harmony or assimilation or mutation of some consonants.

Declension of nouns

Words ending in consonants

Nominative case	El	At	Gül	Ok
Possessive case	Elin	Atın	Gülün	Okun
Dative case	Ele	Ata	Güle	Oka
Objective case	Eli	Atı	Gülü	Oku
Locative case	Elde	Atta	Gülde	Okta
Ablative case	Elden	Attan	Gülden	Oktan

Words ending in vowels

Nominative case	Tilki	Oda	Köprü	Palto
Possessive case	Tilkinin	Odanın	Köprünün	Paltonun
Dative case	Tilkiye	Odaya	Köprüye	Paltoya
Objective case	Tilkiyi	Odayı	Köprüyü	Paltoyu
Locative case	Tilkide	Odada	Köprüde	Paltoda
Ablative case	Tilkiden	Odadan	Köprüden	Paltodan

KEY TO PRONUNCIATION

c (jar), ç (church), g (gale), ğ (lengthen the preceding vowel), h (hill), ı (Cyril), j (Fr. *jeune*), ö (Fr. *peu* or Ger. *Köln*), s (sister), ş (shoe), ü (Fr. *dune* or Ger. *Glück*)

Some essentials of Turkish grammar

All nouns in Turkish are regular in their declension except *su-* (water) which has the irregular possessive form *suyun* instead of the regular form *sunun*.

Varieties of suffixes

El – Hand   Baş – Head

Here are two words, meaning *hand* and *head* respectively. Below are the suffixes that can be attached to these words. These suffixes can be attached to any noun in Turkish, however, one should make sure that to nouns with dominant front vowels the first set should be affixed, while to nouns with dominant back vowels the second set as affixed to Baş.

El-i	his or her hand	Baş-ı	his or her head
El-e	to the hand	Baş-a	to the head
El-de	at or in the hand	Baş-ta	on or in the head
El-den	from the hand	Baş-tan	from the head*
El-im	my hand	Baş-ım	my head
El-in	your hand	Baş-ın	your head
El-imiz	our hand	Baş-ımız	our head
El-iniz	your hand	Baş-ınız	your head
El-leri	their hands	Baş-ları	their heads
El-ler	hands	Baş-lar	heads
El-ceğiz	small hand	Baş-çağız	small head
El-lerin	of the hands	Baş-ların	of the heads
El-lere	to the hands	Baş-lara	to the heads
El-lerde	in the hands	Baş-larda	on or in the heads
El-lerden	out of the hands	Baş-lardan	from or out of the heads
El-lerim	my hands		
El-lerimiz	our hands	Baş-larımız	our heads
El-leriniz	your hands	Baş-larınız	your heads
El-le	by hand	Baş-la	by head, with head
El-siz	without a hand	Baş-sız	without a head†
El-inin	of your hand	Baş-ının	of your head
El-lerinin	of their hands	Baş-larının	of their heads

* Baştan—from the beginning   † Başsız—without a beginning

KEY TO PRONUNCIATION

c (jar), ç (church), g (gale), ğ (lengthen the preceding vowel), h (hill), ı (Cyril), j (Fr. *jeune*), ö (Fr. *peu* or Ger. *Köln*), s (sister), ş (shoe), ü (Fr. *dune* or Ger. *Glück*)

Possessive suffixes

The relationship between two or more nouns, which involves a special construction in Turkish, is called 'Possessive relationship'. If you want to say 'the room of the house' or 'the door of the room' or 'the man's hat' in Turkish, you will have to place the first noun (in this case the house, the room and the man) in the possessive case, ev-in, oda-nın, adam-ın, and the second noun in the objective case, oda-sı, kapısı, şapka-sı. -si, -sı -sü or -su ending replaces the ordinary objective case ending of -i, -ı, –ü or -u when the second noun ends in a vowel instead of a consonant.

The chart for possessive suffixes

	First word Possessive case (of the . . .)	Second word Objective case
Words ending in consonants	-in, ın, -ün, -un	-i, -ı, -ü, -u
Words ending in the consonant (k)	k is replaced by ğ -in, -ın, -ün, -un	k is replaced by ğ -i, -ı, -ü, -u
Words ending in vowels	-nin, -nın, -nün, -nun	-si, -sı, -sü, -su

There are two other forms of possessive relationship. When one of the nouns is a proper noun qualifying the second then the proper noun takes no ending but remains as it is. In the third form, the two nouns take no endings at all. This is when one noun is modifying another to indicate kind, function, origin, or office.

Personal pronouns

Personal pronouns are declined in six cases in Turkish. The different cases serve to take the place of the prepositions 'of', 'to', 'in', 'at', 'from' of English and thus resemble the case-endings of Latin.

KEY TO PRONUNCIATION
c (jar), ç (church), g (gale), ğ (lengthen the preceding vowel), h (hill), ı (Cyril), j (Fr. *jeune*), ö (Fr. *peu* or Ger. *Köln*), s (sister), ş (shoe), ü (Fr. *dune* or Ger. Glück)

Some essentials of Turkish grammar

Personal pronoun chart

Nominative case		Possessive case	Dative case	Objective case	Locative case	Ablative case
ben	I	benim (my)	bana (to me)	beni (me)	bende	benden
sen	thou	senin	sana	seni	sende	senden
o	he, she, it	onun	ona	onu	onda	ondan
biz	we	bizim	bize	bizi	bizde	bizden
siz	you	sizin	size	sizi	sizde	sizden
onlar	they	onların	onlara	onları	onlarda	onlardan

Adjectives

Adjectives in Turkish are placed before the nouns they modify. They are invariable or indeclinable. They retain the same form whatever the number, gender or the case of the noun may be. Examples – güzel Izmir, yeşil Bursa, hasta adam. Comparison of adjectives is expressed by using *daha* and *en* before the adjective—

çok	daha çok	en çok	az	daha az	en az
much	more	most	little	less	least

Adverbs

Adverbs in Turkish are used to limit or complete the meaning of the verb or the adjective. They are adverbs of time, adverbs of place and adverbs of manner.

Adverbs of time		Adverbs of place		Adverbs of manner	
at once	hemen	above	yukarı	almost	hemen hemen
early	erken	back	geri	certainly	tabii
later	sonra	far	uzak	only	yalnız
now	şimdi	inside	içeri	of course	elbette
sometimes	bazan	near	yakın	very	pek

KEY TO PRONUNCIATION

c (jar), ç (church), g (gale), ğ (lengthen the preceding vowel), h (hill), ı (Cyril), j (Fr. *jeune*), ö (Fr. *peu* or Ger. *Köln*), s (sister), ş (shoe), ü (Fr. *dune* or Ger. Glück)

Post-positions

There are no independent prepositions in Turkish that are placed before the nouns to which they refer. These are represented as case-suffixes, attached to the end of the noun. However, there are some post-positions, separate words that follow the noun they refer to. For example: için–for, gibi–like, kadar–as ... as.

Conjunctions

Conjunctions are used to join words, phrases, clauses or sentences. (ve) is used for (and), (fakat) for (but), (çünkü) for (because), etc.

Interjections

Words used to express emotions are called interjections. Here are some of these exclamations:

Come on!	Haydi!	Jolly good!	Aferin!
God willing!	İnşallah!	What a pity!	Yazık!
Long live!	Çok yaşa!	Well done!	Bravo! (Aferin!)
My God!	Vay canına!	Wonderful!	Maşallah!

The Verb

Each Turkish verb is composed of two parts, the verb stem and the infinitive suffix. The infinitive suffix is '-mek' for verbs with front vowels, and '-mak' for verbs with back vowels. When the infinitive suffix of a verb is dropped, you get the imperative of the verb.

Example

to come	gelmek
Come!	Gel!
to sit	oturmak
Sit!	Otur!

A Turkish verb can express itself in all forms and tenses by taking various suffixes without the help of an auxiliary.

Verb conjugation is carried out by dropping the infinitive suffix and by attaching tense suffixes to the stem, to these mood suffixes and finally personal endings are added. Here is an example to illustrate verb conjugation:

KEY TO PRONUNCIATION
c (jar), ç (church), g (gale), ğ (lengthen the preceding vowel), h (hill), ı (Cyril), j (Fr. *jeune*), ö (Fr. *peu* or Ger. *Köln*), s (sister), ş (shoe), ü (Fr. *dune* or Ger. Glück)

Some essentials of Turkish grammar

Gezmek To travel, to go about with a view to seeing things or for enjoyment.

Geziyorum	I am travelling	Gezmişmişim	It is said that I had travelled
Gezerim	I travel		
Gezeceğim	I shall travel	Gezseymişim	It is said that if I had travelled
Gezdim	I travelled		
Gezmişim	It is said that I travelled	Gezeymişim	I wished I had travelled
Gezersem	If I travel	Gezmeliymişim	It is said that I should have travelled
Gezeyim	Let me travel		
Gezmeliyim	I must travel		
Geziyordum	I was travelling	Geziyorsam	If I am travelling
Gezerdim	I used to travel	Gezersem	If I travel
Gezecektim	I was going to travel	Gezeceksem	If I am to travel
		Gezdiysem	If I travelled
Gezdiydim	I had travelled	Gezmişsem	It is said that if I had travelled
Gezmişim	It is said that I have travelled		
		Gezebiliyorum	I can travel
Gezseydim	If I travelled	Gezebilirim	I may travel
Gezeydim	I wish I travelled	Gezebileceğim	I shall be able to travel
Gezmeliydim	I ought to have travelled		
		Gezebildim	I was able to travel
Geziyormuşum	They say that I was travelling	Gezebilmişim	It is said that I was able to travel
Gezermişim	It is said that I travel		
		Gezmekteyim	I am travelling
Gezmiş olacağım	I shall have travelled	Gezmekte olacağım	I shall be travelling
Gezmiş olabilirdim	I could have travelled		
Gezecekmişim	It is said that I would travel		

The personal endings attached to the verb in Turkish are equivalent to the personal pronouns in English. The Turkish verb is never

KEY TO PRONUNCIATION

c (jar), ç (church), g (gale), ğ (lengthen the preceding vowel), h (hill), ı (Cyril), j (Fr. *jeune*), ö (Fr. *peu* or Ger. *Köln*), s (sister), ş (shoe), ü (Fr. *dune* or Ger. Glück)

conjugated without them. It is permissible not to use personal pronouns with Turkish verbs, however they are used for emphasis. It should be borne in mind that there is no specific suffix added to form the third person singular, since the verb-stem with a tense and a mood suffix attached to it, becomes automatically the third person singular of that verb. It is also worth remembering that there is a difference between the second person singular and plural in Turkish. The second person singular is the familiar form, being used among very intimate friends and equals, while the second person plural is used in polite circles and for business purposes.

Personal endings used with various parts of the verb

	Present, future tenses	Past tenses	Imperative
I	-im, -ım, -üm, -um	-m	–
thou	-sin, -sın, -sün, -sun	-n	–
he, she, it	–	–	-sin, -sın, -sün, -sun
we	-iz, -ız, -üz, -uz	-k	–
you	-siniz, -sınız, -sünüz, -sunuz	-niz, -nız, -nüz, -nuz	-in, -ın, -ün, -un -iniz, ınız, -ünüz, -unuz
they	-ler, -lar	-ler, -lar	-sinler, -sınlar, -sünler, -sunlar

The personal endings in the first column are also the verb 'to be' endings in Turkish.

Example

    Zenginim   I am rich
    Zenginsin   Thou art rich
    Zengin   He is rich
    Zenginiz   We are rich
    Zenginsiniz   You are rich
    Zenginler   They are rich

KEY TO PRONUNCIATION

c (jar), ç (church), g (gale), ğ (lengthen the preceding vowel), h (hill), ı (Cyril), j (Fr. *jeune*), ö (Fr. *peu* or Germ. *Köln*), s (sister), ş (shoe), ü (Fr. *dune* or Ger. Glück)

Some essentials of Turkish grammar

Forms of the verb

Negative, interrogative and negative interrogative forms of the verb are formed by suffixes which are placed between the verb stem and the personal endings. The negative particle is '-me' or '-ma' with one or two exceptions. The interrogative particle is 'mi', 'mı', 'mü', or 'mu'. Unlike the negative sign this is not joined to the word it follows, but stands by itself. Both the negative particle and the interrogative particle are not stressed in Turkish, therefore the stress falls on the syllable preceding the particles.

An affirmative statement can be made interrogative by placing after it the negative of the verb 'to be' which is 'değil mi?' similar to the French 'n'est ce pas'.

Examples

Verdim	I gave	Vermedim	I did not give
Verdim mi?	Did I give?	Vermedim mi?	Did I not give?

Verdim, değil mi? I gave, didn't I?

The Turkish language has no special verb as 'to have' in English or 'avoir' in French. The meaning of such a verb is expressed in an entirely different manner, by using the special verb 'var' together with the possessive case of the personal pronouns. On the other hand 'yok' is used for 'not to have' in the same construction as for 'to have' for the negative.

Examples

Benim iki bavulum var   I have two pieces of luggage
Onun bir çantası var   He has one brief-case

'Etmek' and 'Olmak' are two of the main auxiliary verbs in Turkish. 'Etmek' means 'to do', 'to perform', and 'olmak' means 'to become'.

Example

Teşekkür etmek	to thank
Telefon etmek	to telephone
Hizmet etmek	to serve
Hasta olmak	to become ill

KEY TO PRONUNCIATION
c (jar), ç (church), g (gale), ğ (lengthen the preceding vowel), h (hill), ı (Cyril), j (Fr. *jeune*), ö (Fr. *peu* or Ger. *Köln*), s (sister), ş (shoe), ü (Fr. *dune* or Ger. Glück)

3 Useful expressions

Important Phrases

Yes.	Evet.
No.	Hayır.
Please!	Lütfen!
Thank you!	Teşekkür ederim!
When?	Ne zaman?
At what time?	Saat kaçta?
Where is ...?	... nerededir?
Is it near here?	Buraya yakın mı?
Where can I buy ...?	... nereden satın alabilirim?
How much is this?	Bu kaçadır?
Is there anything cheaper?	Dahu ucuzu var mı?
Isn't there anything better?	Daha iyisi yok mu?
I want to go to ...	... 'e gitmek istiyorum.
Do you go to ...?	... 'e gidiyor musunuz?
Please bring me ...	Lütfen bana ... getiriniz.
When does it open?	Ne zaman açılır?
When does it close?	Ne zaman kapanır?
Which is the way to ...?	... 'e hangi yoldan gidilir?
How far is it?	Ne kadar uzaktır?
How long does it take?	Ne kadar sürer?
When do we arrive at ...?	... 'e ne zaman varıyoruz?
When do we leave?	Ne zaman yola çıkıyoruz?
Is there ...?	... var mı?
Have you got ...?	Sizde bulunur mu?
Sorry!	Pardon!

KEY TO PRONUNCIATION

c (jar), ç (church), g (gale), ğ (lengthen the preceding vowel), h (hill), ı (Cyril), j (Fr. *jeune*), ö (Fr. *peu* or Ger. *Köln*), s (sister), ş (shoe), ü (Fr. *dune* or Ger. Glück)

Useful expressions

Excuse me!	Affedersiniz!
All right!	Olur, peki!
A little!	Biraz.
Small.	Küçük.
Big.	Büyük.
Cheap	Ucuz.
Expensive.	Pahalı.
Quickly.	Çabuk.
Slowly.	Yavaş.
Listen!	Dinle!
Look!	Bak!
How lovely.	Ne güzel!
Like this.	Bunun gibi.
Look out!	Dikkat!
Watch your step!	Önüne bak!
Wait here.	Burada bekle.
I don't know.	Bilmiyorum.
This doesn't work.	Bu işlemiyor.
This is out of order.	Bu bozuk.
I don't understand.	Anlamıyorum.
You are right.	Haklısınız.
You are wrong.	Haksızsınız.
Whose turn is it?	Kimin sırası?
What is the matter?	Ne var?
What is that?	O nedir?
What is the news?	Ne var, ne yok?

Turkish, refined by the Ottoman Turks for the past six centuries, has considerably more set expressions for particular occasions than any other living language. Not only are there elaborate phrases for welcoming a guest, seeing him off, apologizing, but there are quite a number of others for wishing him recovery, congratulating him, wishing him luck and bidding farewell. Learning and using some of these will make a great deal of difference on your trip to Turkey.

KEY TO PRONUNCIATION

c (jar), ç (church), g (gale), ğ (lengthen the preceding vowel), h (hill), ı (Cyril), j (Fr. *jeune*), ö (Fr. *peu* or Ger. *Köln*), s (sister), ş (shoe), ü (Fr. *dune* or Ger. Glück)

Greetings and leave-takings

Hello!	Merhaba!
Good morning!	Günaydın!
How do you do!	Nasılsınız!
Welcome to Turkey!	Türkiyeye hoşgeldiniz!
Do come in!	İçeri buyrunuz!
Step in, please!	Buyrun, lütfen!
How are you?	Nasılsınız?
Very well, thank you, and you?	İyiyim, teşekkür ederim, ya siz?
Pleased to meet you!	Tanıştığımıza memnun oldum.
That honour is mine!	O şeref bana ait!
What a surprise to see you after all these years!	Seneler sonra sizi görmek ne büyük bir sürpriz!
Let us keep in touch this time.	Bu sefer, teması kaybetmiyelim.
Pleasant journey!	İyi yolculuklar!
Keep well!	Esen kal!
So long!	Hoşça kalınız!
Good-bye!	Allahasmarladık! (Said by person leaving.)
Good-bye!	Güle güle! (Said by person who is seeing his friend off.)
Good-night!	İyi geceler!

Thanks

Please.	Lütfen.
Thank you.	Teşekkür ederim.
Thanks!	Teşekkürler!
I am very grateful to you.	Size müteşekkirim.
I am deeply indebted to you.	Size son derece minnettarım.
You are very kind.	Çok naziksiniz.
It doesn't matter.	Bir ziyanı yok.
Don't mention it.	Bir şey değil.
Thank you for the interest you have shown.	Gösterdiğiniz ilgiye teşekkür ederim.

KEY TO PRONUNCIATION

c (jar), ç (church), g (gale), ğ (lengthen the preceding vowel), h (hill), ı (Cyril), j (Fr. *jeune*), ö (Fr. *peu* or Ger. *Köln*), s (sister), ş (shoe), ü (Fr. *dune* or Ger. Glück)

Useful expressions

Thank you for the trouble.	Zahmetinize teşekkürler.
I should like to thank you for your present.	Hediyenize teşekkür etmek isterim!
I won't forget your kindness.	Bu iyiliğinizi hiç unutmıyacağım.
A thousand thanks for your hospitality!	Misafirperverliğinize binlerce teşekkürler!

Requests

Please sit down.	Lütfen oturunuz.
Do take a seat.	Oturunuz, lütfen.
May I ask you a favour?	Bir recada bulunabilir miyim?
Can you help me?	Bana yardım edebilir misiniz?
I have a request to make.	Bir recam var.
Just a minute, please!	Bir dakika, lütfen!
If it is not much bother.	Zahmet olmazsa.
With pleasure!	Memnuniyetle!
It is a pleasure!	Bir zevktir. (Zevk olur!)
Please do not disturb me.	Lütfen beni rahatsız etmeyiniz.
What do you want?	Ne istiyorsunuz?
Can I help you?	Size yardım edebilir miyim?
After you!	Sizden sonra! (Siz buyurun!)

Regrets

I beg your pardon.	Affedersiniz. (Pardon.)
Sorry, I apologize.	Özür dilerim!
Excuse me.	Affedersiniz.
Please forgive me!	Lütfen, beni affediniz!
I did not want to hurt your feelings.	Hislerinizi incitmek istemedim.
Please accept my regrets.	Lütfen suçumu bağışlayın.
Please don't take it seriously.	Lütfen ciddiye almayın.
I should like to make it up with you.	Gönlünüzü almak isterim.
It was not intentional.	Kasden yapmadım.

KEY TO PRONUNCIATION
c (jar), ç (church), g (gale), ğ (lengthen the preceding vowel), h (hill), ı (Cyril), j (Fr. *jeune*), ö (Fr. *peu* or Ger. *Köln*), s (sister), ş (shoe), ü (Fr. *dune* or Ger. Glück)

Wishes

Good appetite!	Afiyet olsun! (Before eating.)
Be in health, *or* be alive!	Sağ ol! (To show gratitude, stronger than thank you!)
May you recover soon!	Geçmiş olsun! (To someone who is ill – get well.)
Never mind!	Sağlık olsun!
To your good health!	Sıhhatinize! (When raising your glass.)
Cheers! (Skal! Prosit!)	Şerefinize! (When raising your glass.)
I congratulate you.	Sizi tebrik ederim.
Congratulations!	Tebrikler!
May God be content with you, we enjoyed ourselves.	Allah sizden razı olsun, iyi eğlendik.
Wear it in good health!	Güle güle giyiniz! (To someone who appears in a new dress, suit, shoes, etc.)
To many years!	Nice senelere! (Congratulating a person on his birthday or on New Year's Day.)
Many happy returns!	
And to you too!	Size de!
Good health to you!	Sıhhatler olsun! (Said to one having had a bath or a shave.)
Have a long married life.	Bir yastıkta kocayınız.
Please accept my condolences.	Başınız sağ olsun.
May it be easy.	Kolay gelsin. (Said to someone at work.)
May your hands be always in health!	Elinize sağlık! (Thanking someone who has accomplished a feat with his or her hands.)

Enquiries and difficulties

Will you allow me?	Müsaade eder misiniz?
Will you help me?	Bana yardım eder misiniz?

KEY TO PRONUNCIATION

c (jar), ç (church), g (gale), ğ (lengthen the preceding vowel), h (hill), ı (Cyril), j (Fr. *jeune*), ö (Fr. *peu* or Ger. *Köln*), s (sister), ş (shoe), ü (Fr. *dune* or Ger. *Glück*)

Useful expressions

Who are you?	Siz kimsiniz?
What do you want?	Ne istiyorsunuz?
Do you speak ...?	... konuşur musunuz?
Will you repeat it, please?	Lütfen tekrarlar mısınız?
Does anyone here speak English?	Burada İngilizce konuşan var mı?
Where is the station?	Istasyon nerede?
Where is the best hotel?	En iyi otel nerede?
Where are we going?	Nereye gidiyoruz?
Where are you taking me?	Beni nereye götürüyorsunuz?
Where are you going?	Nereye gidiyorsunuz?
Where can I telephone?	Nereden telefon edebilirim?
Where is the lift?	Asansör ne tarafta?
Can you direct me to ...?	... gösterebilir misiniz?
Is there a bus stop near here?	Yakında bir otobüs durağı var mı?
Where can I change money?	Nerede para bozdurabilirim?
Can you give me information?	Bana bilgi verebilir misiniz?
What time is it?	Saat kaç?
I am English.	Ben İngilizim.
I am American.	Ben Amerikalıyım.
I am looking for ...	... arıyorum.
Speak slowly, please.	Lütfen yavaş konuşunuz.
I can't understand you.	Sizi anlıyamıyorum.
I don't know Turkish.	Türkçe bilmiyorum.
Let me look for the phrase.	Cümleyi arıyayım.
Please come here.	Lütfen buraya geliniz.
Please read this.	Lütfen bunu okuyunuz.
Come and see!	Gel ve gör!
Help!	Imdat!
Please help me!	Lütfen bana yardım ediniz!
Please, leave me alone!	Lütfen beni rahat bırakınız!
Please call a policeman!	Lütfen bir polis çağırınız!
Please call an ambulance!	Lütfen bir cankurtaran çağırınız!
I don't know you.	Sizi tanımıyorum.
I don't want to speak to you.	Sizinle konuşmak istemiyorum.

KEY TO PRONUNCIATION
c (jar), ç (church), g (gale), ğ (lengthen the preceding vowel), h (hill), ı (Cyril), j (Fr. *jeune*), ö (Fr. *peu* or Ger. *Köln*), s (sister), ş (shoe), ü (Fr. *dune* or Ger. Glück)

Useful expressions

You are making a mistake.	Hata ediyorsunuz.
It was not me.	Ben değildim.
He is a thief!	Hırsız var!
Catch him!	Yakalayın!
There is a fire!	Yangın var!
It doesn't interest me.	Beni ilgilendirmez.
Let me pass!	Bırak geçeyim!
I need an interpreter.	Bir tercümana ihtiyacım var.
I can't explain myself	İstediğimi anlatamıyorum.
I have got a complaint to make.	Bir şikâyetim var.
Where is the British Consulate?	İngiliz konsolosluğu nerede?
Where is the American Consulate?	Amerikan konsolosluğu nerede?
To whom should I apply?	Kime başvurayım?
I want the police to investigate.	Polisin araştırma yapmasını istiyorum.
What does that mean?	O ne demek?
I have paid you enough.	Paranı verdim ya.
I shall report you to the police.	Seni polise şikâyet edeceğim.
You will be sorry for this!	Sonra pişman olacaksın!
I'll make you pay for this!	Gösteririm sana!
This is very annoying.	Bu çok can sıkıcı bir şey.
Have I done anything wrong?	Yanlış bir şey mi yaptım?
I have done nothing.	Hiç bir şey yapmadım.
I didn't do it.	Onu ben yapmadım.
It has nothing to do with me.	Benimle hiç bir ilgisi yok.
Must I get a permit to work?	Çalışma müsaadesi almam lazım mı?
I can only speak a little Turkish.	Pek az Türkçe biliyorum.
I can read it, but I cannot speak it.	Okuyabiliyorum ama konuşamıyorum.

Notices

Admission	Giriş, Duhuliye	Bus stop	Otobüs Durağı, Durak
Alarm signal	Tehlike işareti		
Bathroom	Banyo	Closed	Kapalı

KEY TO PRONUNCIATION

c (jar), ç (church), g (gale), ğ (lengthen the preceding vowel), h (hill), ı (Cyril), j (Fr. *jeune*), ö (Fr. *peu* or Ger. *Köln*), s (sister), ş (shoe), ü (Fr. *dune* or Ger. *Glück*)

Useful expressions

Cold	Soğuk	Museum	Müze
Cross	Geç	Occupied	Meşgul, dolu
Danger	Tehlike	Open	Açık
Dining-room	Yemek salonu, Restoran	Proceed	Yürü, ilerle!
		Pull!	Çekiniz!
Entrance	Giriş	Push!	İtiniz!
Exit	Çıkış	Shared taxi	Dolmuş
Forbidden	Yasak	Smoking	Sigara içmek
For ladies	Bayanlara, kadınlara	Spitting	Tükürmek
		Stop!	Dur!
For gentlemen	Baylara, erkeklere	Telephone	Telefon
		Ticket	Bilet
For rent	Kiralık	Ticket office	Gişe
For sale	Satılık	Waiting-room	Bekleme Salonu
Free	Serbest, boş	Warm	Sıcak
Gentlemen	Baylar, erkekler	Writing-room	Yazı salonu
Go slowly!	Yavaş gidiniz!	W.C.	Tuvalet, aptesane, Yüz numara
Ladies	Bayanlar, kadınlar		
Lavatory	W.C., Yüz numara, Tuvalet		

Regulatory signs

Attention	Dikkat
Dangerous cross-roads	Tehlikeli yol kavşağı
Do not pass	Geçmek yasaktır
Do not stop	Durmak yasaktır
Direction to be followed	Mecburi istikamet
Keep to the right	Sağdan gidiniz
Level crossing	Tren yolu geçidi
Load limit	Azami ağırlık
No entry for lorries	Kamyon giremez
No entry for motor vehicles	Motörlü taşıt giremez
No entry for vehicles	Taşıt giremez

KEY TO PRONUNCIATION

c (jar), ç (church), g (gale), ğ (lengthen the preceding vowel), h (hill), ı (Cyril), j (Fr. *jeune*), ö (Fr. *peu* or Ger. *Köln*), s (sister), ş (shoe), ü (Fr. *dune* or Ger. *Glück*)

Useful expressions

No left turn	Sola dönülmez
No horn blowing	Klakson çalınmaz
No parking	Park yapılmaz
No U turn	Geri dönülmez
One way	Tek yön
Parking limited one hour	Azami park 1 saat
Road closed	Yol kapalı
Sharp corner	Keskin viraj
Speed limit	Azami sürat
Slow	Yavaş

Traffic signs

Axle weight limit	Azami dingil ağırlığı
Bend	Viraj, dönemeç
Bends	Devamlı virajlar
Camping site	Kamp yeri
Caravan site	Römorklu kamp yeri
Crossing with gates	Kapanır geçit
Dangerous hill	Tehlikeli eğim
Direction to be followed	Mecburi yön
End of no overtaking	Geçme yasağı sonu
Entering traffic	Yandan giriş
Falling rocks	Gevşek şev
Filling station	Akar yakıt, benzin istasyonu
Give way	Yol ver
Give way to oncoming traffic	Karşıdan gelene yol ver
Loose gravel	Gevşek malzeme
Minor road junction	Tali yol kavşağı
Minimum speed	Asgari hız
No entry	Taşıt giremez
No overtaking	Geçme yasağı
No right turn	Sağa dönülmez
Opening bridge	Açılan köprü
Pedestrian crossing	Yaya geçidi

KEY TO PRONUNCIATION

c (jar), ç (church), g (gale), ğ (lengthen the preceding vowel), h (hill), ı (Cyril), j (Fr. *jeune*), ö (Fr. *peu* or Germ. *Köln*), s (sister), ş (shoe), ü (Fr. *dune* or Ger. Glück)

Useful expressions

Reverse curve	Sağa zikzak
Road junction	Kavşak
Road narrows	Daralan kaplama
Road works	Yolda çalışma
Roundabout	Dönel kavşak
School-children	Okul
Slippery road	Kaygan yol
Stop – customs	Gümrük
Stop – police	Polis
Traffic signals	Işıklı işaret
Two way traffic	İki yönlü trafik
Uneven road	Kasis

KEY TO PRONUNCIATION

c (jar), ç (church), g (gale), ğ (lengthen the preceding vowel), h (hill), ı (Cyril), j (Fr. *jeune*), ö (Fr. *peu* or Ger. *Köln*), s (sister), ş (shoe), ü (Fr. *dune* or Ger. *Glück*)

4 Money

In Turkey, the basic unit of currency is the 'lira', which is divided into '100 kuruş'. In English, lira is called the Turkish Pound and Kuruş is named piastre. Banknotes are of 10, 20, 50, 100, 500, 1,000, 5,000, and 10,000 liras. Coins are of 1, 5, and 10 Turkish liras.

The lira is equal to 100 kuruş. The value of the Turkish pound against European currencies is determined daily by the Turkish Central Bank. The import of foreign currency into Turkey is not restricted. Tourists arriving in Turkey may carry Turkish currency up to the value of 100 US dollars. You may convert your traveller's cheques and foreign currency into Turkish lira wherever you wish. Eurocheques as well as traveller's cheques can be cashed immediately upon producing identification. However, it may take several days to clear cheques from private accounts because the relevant bank abroad has to be contacted. Should you desire to change your liras into pounds on your departure, you should ask for a receipt when having them converted, and present this exchange slip to the bank entitled to deal in foreign currency.

Tourists are free to take out any currency they have brought into the country. However, they are permitted to take Turkish currency only up to the equivalent of 100 US dollars with them.

Besides their personal belongings and jewellery, tourists are entitled to take home with them souvenirs, gifts up to the value of 1,000 US dollars in Turkish currency. Gifts exceeding this sum should be accompanied by an exchange slip as proof of conversion of your currency into Turkish pounds.

All prices given in this book are approximate and subject to change.

Money

Vocabulary

account	hesap	letter of credit	akreditif
altitude	rakım, yükseklik	loss	zarar
		measure	ölçü
bank	banka	money	para
bill	kağıt para	open an account	hesap açmak
cash, to	paraya çevirmek	piastre	kuruş
cashier	kasadar, veznedar	pound	sterlin
change, to	para bozmak	profit	kâr
change	bozuk para	quarter	çeyrek
cheque	çek	rate	rayiç, değer
coin	sikke, ufaklık	rate of exchange	kambiyo rayici
current account	cari hesap	share	hisse senedi
depth	derinlik	sign, to	imzalamak
deposit account	depozito hesabı	temperature	ısı derecesi
distance	mesafe	thickness	kalınlık
exchange	kambiyo	third	üçüncü
exchange, to	değiştirmek	three	üç
half	yarım, yarı	three-quarters	üç çeyrek
height	yükseklik	two-thirds	üçte iki
interest	faiz	weight	ağırlık
length	uzunluk	width	en, genişlik

Phrases

Is this a bank?	Burası banka mıdır?
Is there a bank near here?	Yakında bir banka var mı?
Which is the counter dealing with foreign exchange?	Kambiyo (Foreign Exchange) masası ne tarafta?
Where is the cashier's office?	Vezne nerede?
Where can one cash this cheque?	Bu çeki nerede bozdurabilirim?
Where can I cash this traveller's cheque?	Travelers çeki nerede bozdurabilirim?
Will you cash this cheque?	Bu çeki bozabilir misiniz?
You have forgotten your signature.	İmzanızı unutmuşsunuz.

KEY TO PRONUNCIATION
c (jar), ç (church), g (gale), ğ (lengthen the preceding vowel), h (hill), ı (Cyril), j (Fr. *jeune*), ö (Fr. *peu* or Ger. *Köln*), s (sister), ş (shoe), ü (Fr. *dune* or Ger. Glück)

Money

Where must I sign?	Nereyi imzalamalıyım?
Can I exchange these pounds?	Bu sterlinleri bozdurabilir miyim?
Can I exchange these dollars?	Bu doları bozdurabilir miyim?
What is the rate of exchange for pounds today?	Sterlinin bugünkü kuru nedir?
Would you please exchange these for me?	Lütfen bunları Türk parasına çevirebilir misiniz?
How much is that worth?	O ne kadar eder?
I have a letter of credit.	Bir kredi mektubum var. (Akreditifim var.)
Can you give me some small change for five liras?	Bana beş liralık bozuk para verebilir misiniz?
Are you sure about your calculations?	Hesabınızdan emin misiniz acaba?
Would you please check your calculations?	Lütfen hesabınızı bir kere daha kontrol eder misiniz?
How much commission do you charge?	Ne kadar komisyon alıyorsunuz?
Thank you for re-checking.	Kontrolünüz için teşekkür ederim.

Numbers

Cardinal numbers

1	bir		10	on
2	iki		11	onbir
3	üç		12	oniki
4	dört		13	onüç
5	beş		14	ondört
6	altı		15	onbeş
7	yedi		16	onaltı
8	sekiz		17	onyedi
9	dokuz		18	onsekiz

KEY TO PRONUNCIATION

c (jar), ç (church), g (gale), ğ (lengthen the preceding vowel), h (hill), ı (Cyril), j (Fr. *jeune*), ö (Fr. *peu* or Ger. *Köln*), s (sister), ş (shoe), ü (Fr. *dune* or Ger. Glück)

Money

19	ondokuz	400	dörtyüz
20	yirmi	500	beşyüz
21	yirmibir	600	altıyüz
22	yirmiiki	700	yediyüz
23	yirmiüç	800	sekizyüz
24	yirmidört	900	dokuzyüz
25	yirmibeş	1,000	bin
26	yirmialtı	1,001	binbir
27	yirmiyedi	1,051	binellibir
28	yirmisekiz	2,000	ikibin
29	yirmidokuz	3,000	üçbin
30	otuz	4,000	dörtbin
40	kırk	5,000	beşbin
50	elli	10,000	onbin
60	altmış	100,000	yüzbin
70	yetmiş	500,000	Beşyüzbin, yarım milyon
80	seksen		
90	doksan	800,000	sekizyüzbin
100	yüz	900,000	dokuzyüzbin
200	ikiyüz	950,000	dokuzyüzellibin
300	üçyüz	1,000,000	bir milyon

Ordinal numbers

1st	birinci
2nd	ikinci
3rd	üçüncü
4th	dördüncü
5th	beşinci
6th	altıncı
7th	yedinci
8th	sekizinci
9th	dokuzuncu
10th	onuncu

Distributive numbers

one each, in ones	birer
two each, in twos	ikişer
three each	üçer
four each	dörder
five each	beşer
six each, in sixes	altışar
seven each	yedişer
eight each	sekizer
nine each	dokuzar
ten each, in tens	onar

KEY TO PRONUNCIATION

c (jar), ç (church), g (gale), ğ (lengthen the preceding vowel), h (hill), ı (Cyril), j (Fr. *jeune*), ö (Fr. *peu* or Ger. *Köln*), s (sister), ş (shoe), ü (Fr. *dune* or Ger. Glück)

Years

1939	bin dokuzyüz otuzdokuz
1968	bin dokuzyüz altmışsekiz
1971	bin dokuzyüz yetmişbir
1984	bin dokuzyüz seksendört

Proportional numbers

1/2	yarım	4/7	yedide dört
1/3	üçte bir	1/10	onda bir
2/3	üçte iki	10/100	yüzde on
2/5	beşte iki	12/1000	binde oniki
3/4	dörtte üç		

Phrases

What do I owe you?	Size ne kadar borcum var?
I have no change on me.	Üzerimde bozuk para yok!
How far is it from here?	Buradan ne kadar mesafede?
It is 33 kilometres from here.	Buradan otuzüç kilometre mesafede
How long will it take me to get there?	Oraya gitmek ne kadar sürer?
It will take you about an hour if you walk.	Yürürseniz bir saatte gidersiniz.
Is this the last day of your holidays?	Tatilinizin son günü mü?
I want to take a few days off.	Bir kaç gün izin almak istiyorum.
Can you lend me some money?	Bana bir az borç para verebilir misiniz?
When can you repay me?	Ne zaman iade edebilirsiniz?
I am expecting some money any day now.	Her an paramın gelmesini bekliyorum.
May I defer payment until next Friday?	Gelecek Cumaya kadar ödemesem olur mu?
Is the tax deducted from your salary?	Maaşınızdan vergi kesilir mi?

KEY TO PRONUNCIATION

c (jar), ç (church), g (gale), ğ (lengthen the preceding vowel), h (hill), ı (Cyril), j (Fr. *jeune*), ö (Fr. *peu* or Ger. *Köln*), s (sister), ş (shoe), ü (Fr. *dune* or Ger. *Glück*)

Money

How much commission do you pay when you change foreign currency?	Yabancı para (döviz) bozdurduğunuz zaman ne komisyon ödüyorsunuz?
Will you take my measurements for a suit?	Elbise için ölçülerimi alır mısınız?
The cloth is three metres long.	Kumaş üç metredir.
Do you make shoes to measure?	Ismarlama ayakkabı yapıyor musunuz?
How long have you been waiting?	Ne zamandaberi bekliyorsunuz?
More than half an hour!	Yarım saatten fazla!

Conversion tables

Distance

Kilometres	Miles or Kilometres	Miles
1·6	1	0·6
3·2	2	1·2
4·8	3	1·9
6·4	4	2·5
8·1	5	3·1
9·7	6	3·7
11·3	7	4·4
12·9	8	5·0
14·5	9	5·6
16·1	10	6·2
32·3	20	12·4
40·2	25	15·3
80·5	50	31·1
128·7	80	50·0
160·9	100	62·1
321·9	200	124·3
643·7	400	248·5
804·7	500	310·7

To convert miles to kilometres divide by 5 and multiply by 8.
To convert from kilometres to miles divide by 8 and multiply by 5.

KEY TO PRONUNCIATION

c (jar), ç (church), g (gale), ğ (lengthen the preceding vowel), h (hill), ı (Cyril), j (Fr. *jeune*), ö (Fr. *peu* or Ger. *Köln*), s (sister), ş (shoe), ü (Fr. *dune* or Ger. *Glück*)

Length

Centimetres	Inches or centimetres	Inches
2·5	1	0·4
5·1	2	0·8
7·6	3	1·2
10·2	4	1·6
12·7	5	2·0
15·2	6	2·4
17·8	7	2·8
20·0	8	3·2
22·9	9	3·5
25·4	10	3·9
50·8	20	7·9
63·5	25	9·8
127·0	50	19·7
254·0	100	39·4

To convert from inches to centimetres divide by 2 and multiply by 5.
To convert from centimetres to inches divide by 5 and multiply by 2.

Altitude

Metres	Feet or Metres	Feet
0·3	1	3·3
0·6	2	6·6
0·9	3	9·8
1·2	4	13·1
1·5	5	16·4
1·8	6	19·7
2·1	7	23·0
2·4	8	26·3
2·7	9	29·5
3·0	10	32·8
6·1	20	65·6
7·6	25	82·0
15·2	50	164·0
30·5	100	328·1

To convert from feet to metres divide by 10 and multiply by 3.
To convert from metres to feet divide by 3 and multiply by 10.

In certain instances you may be confronted with yards instead of metres, to convert from one to the other, is very simple. In order to convert from yards to metres, you divide by 10 and multiply by 9, and to convert from metres to yards, you divide by 9 and multiply by 10.

Weight

Grammes	Ounces	Ounces	Grammes
100	3·5	2	57·1
250	8·8	4	114·3
500	17·6	8	228·6
1,000 (1kg.)	35·0	16	457·2

To convert from ounces to grammes divide by 7 and multiply by 200, and from grammes to ounces, divide by 200 and multiply by 7.

Kilogrammes	Lb or Kg	Pounds
0·5	1	2·2
0·9	2	4·4
1·4	3	6·6
1·8	4	8·8
2·3	5	11·0
4·5	10	22·1
11·3	25	55·1
22·7	50	110·2

To convert from lbs. to kgs., divide by 11 and multiply by 5, and to convert from kgs. to lbs., divide by 5 and multiply by 11.

Pressure

lbs./sq. in.	kg./sq. cm.	kg./sq. cm.	lbs./sq. in.
16	approx. 1·12	1·1	approx. 16·0
18	1·27	1·3	18·5
20	1·41	1·4	19·9
22	1·55	1·6	22·8
24	1·69	1·7	24·2
26	1·83	1·8	25·6
28	1·97	2·0	28·4
30	2·11	2·1	29·9

Temperature

Fahrenheit (F)	Centigrade (C)	Fahrenheit (F)	Centigrade (C)
212 (boiling)	100	80	26·7
104	40	77	25
102	38·9	68	20
101	38·3	64	17·8
100	37·8	59	15
98·4 (body)	37	50	10
97	36·1	41	5
86	30	32 (freezing)	0

Clothing sizes

Dresses and suits (women)

British	32	34	36	38	40	42
American	10	12	14	16	18	20
Continental	38	40	42	44	46	48

Suits and Overcoats (men)

British and American	36	38	40	42	44	46
Continental	46	48	50	52	54	56

Shirts

British and American	14	14·5	15	15·5	16	16·5	17
Continental	36	37	38	39	41	42	43

Shoes

British	5	6	7	8	9	10	11	12
American	6·5	7·5	8·5	9·5	10·5	11·5	12·5	13·5
Continental	38	39/40	41	42	43	44	45	46

Socks

British and American	9·5	10	10·5	11	11·5
Continental	38–39	39–40	40–41	41–42	42–43

Stockings

British and American	8	8·5	9	9·5	10	10·5	11
Continental	0	1	2	3	4	5	6

Hats

British and American	6·5	$6\frac{5}{8}$	$6\frac{3}{4}$	$6\frac{7}{8}$	7	$7\frac{1}{8}$
Continental	53	54	55	56	57	58

Money

Tipping

It is customary to give gratuities in Turkey for services rendered in hotels, restaurants, cafés and theatres. The porters of the de luxe hotels usually get a tip of 50 – 100 Turkish liras per trip. The person who cleans the room gets 100 Tl. for a couple of days and 500 Tl. for a week. The desk clerk gets twice as much as the person who cleans the room. Hotel barbers are tipped 100 Tl. and ladies' hairdressers 150 – 200 Tl. A theatre or a cinema usher gets 50 Tl. per party. A service charge is normally included in all hotel and restaurant bills but it is also usual to give a tip of 10 per cent of the total amount charged. Taxi drivers expect 10 per cent on amount charged.

Conversion table

Since the Turkish lira is a floating currency and its value against other European currencies is determined daily by the Central Bank of Turkey, it is difficult to set a conversion table. Therefore, it would be advisable to get in touch with one of the foremost commercial banks of Turkey, the Iş Bank's London Branch at 21 Aldermanbury, London EC2P 2BY. Telephone (01) 606 7151, before your departure, to find out the value of your pound in Turkey.

5 Time

Time in Turkey is Greenwich Mean Time plus two. With the adoption of summer time the difference between England and Turkey falls to one hour.

Vocabulary

after	sonra	following day	ertesi gün
afternoon	öğleden sonra, ikindi	fortnight	onbeş gün, iki hafta
alarm-clock	çalar saat	half	buçuk
always	herzaman	half past twelve	yarım
at one time	vaktiyle	hour	saat
at once	derhal	immediately	derhal
before	evvel, önce	last	son, geçen
beginning	baş, başlangıç	late	geç
calendar	takvim	midday	öğle
century	yüzyıl, asır	midnight	gece yarısı
clock	dıvar saati	minute	dakika
date	tarih, gün	month	ay
day	gün	morning	sabah
day before	evvelki gün	never	asla, hiç bir zaman
during	esnasında, sırasında		
		New Year's Day	yılbaşı günü
early	erken	next day	ertesi gün
end	son	night	gece
evening	akşam	now	şimdi
first	ilk, birinci	often	çok zaman

KEY TO PRONUNCIATION
c (jar), ç (church), g (gale), ğ (lengthen the preceding vowel), h (hill), ı (Cyril), j (Fr. *jeune*), ö (Fr. *peu* or Ger. *Köln*), s (sister), ş (shoe), ü (Fr. *dune* or Ger. *Glück*)

Time

quarter	çeyrek (çeyrek saat, onbeş dakika)	this morning	bu sabah
		today	bugün
		tomorrow	yarın
round about	sularında	tonight	bu gece
season	mevsim	wrist-watch	kol saati
second	saniye	week	hafta
sometimes	bazan	year	yıl, sene
soon	hemen	yesterday	dün
then	o zaman		

Days of the week

Sunday	Pazar	Thursday	Perşembe
Monday	Pazartesi	Friday	Cuma
Tuesday	Salı	Saturday	Cumartesi
Wednesday	Çarşamba		

Time expressions

During the morning	Sabahleyin	Every day	Hergün
		Daily	Günlük
During the day	Gündüzün	All day	Bütün gün
At night	Geceleyin	Night and day	Gece gündüz
This evening	Bu akşam	Last week	Geçen hafta
Last night	Dün gece	Next week	Gelecek hafta
Yesterday morning	Dün sabah	Last Friday	Geçen Cuma
		Next Sunday	Gelecek Pazar
Tomorrow morning	Yarın sabah	A week today	Gelecek hafta bugün, haftaya bugün
The day after tomorrow	Öbürgün		
		A week ago	Geçen hafta
The day before yesterday	Evvelsi gün	This month	Bu ay
		Next month	Gelecek ay

KEY TO PRONUNCIATION

c (jar), ç (church), g (gale), ğ (lengthen the preceding vowel), h (hill), ı (Cyril), j (Fr. *jeune*), ö (Fr. *peu* or Ger. *Köln*), s (sister), ş (shoe), ü (Fr. *dune* or Ger. Glück)

Last month	Geçen ay	Frequently	Sık sık
A holiday	Bayram, tatil günü	Yet, still	Henüz
		Up till now	Hala
Christmas	Noel	Once	Bir zamanlar
New Year's day	Yılbaşı günü	In the past	Vaktiyle
Easter	Paskalya	At last, finally	Nihayet
Now and then	Arasıra		

Months and seasons

January	Ocak	July	Temmuz
February	Şubat	August	Ağustos
March	Mart	September	Eylül
April	Nisan	October	Ekim
May	Mayıs	November	Kasım
June	Haziran	December	Aralık
spring	ilkbahar	autumn	sonbahar
summer	yaz	winter	kış

Phrases

How long have you been here?	Ne zamandanberi buradasınız?
I have been here a month.	Bir aydanberi buradayım.
I have been here since last summer.	Geçen yazdanberi buradayım.
I have been here since 17 May.	17 Mayıstanberi buradayım.
What is the date today?	Bugünün tarihi ne? (Bugün ayın kaçı.)
It is 23 April.	23 Nisandır.
22 June.	22 Haziran.
When will the plane take off?	Uçak ne zaman havalanacak?
It will take off at 14.30.	Saat ondört otuzda havalanacak. (Saat ikibuçukta havalanacak.)
At what time does the train leave?	Tren saat kaçta kalkıyor?
At ten past nine.	Saat dokuzu on geçe.

KEY TO PRONUNCIATION

c (jar), ç (church), g (gale), ğ (lengthen the preceding vowel), h (hill), ı (Cyril), j(Fr. *jeune*), ö (Fr. *peu* or Ger. *Köln*), s (sister), ş (shoe), ü (Fr. *dune* or Ger. *Glück*)

Time

When did you receive the telegram?	Telgrafı ne zaman aldınız?
At four p.m.	Saat dörtte.
Up to what time?	Ne zamana kadar?
From morning till evening.	Sabahtan akşama kadar.
When will it be ready?	Ne zaman hazır olacak?
It will be ready by tomorrow.	Yarına kadar hazırdır.
As far as where are we going?	Nereye kadar gideceğiz?
I am going to wait till five o'clock.	Saat beşe kadar bekliyorum.
How long does it take to go to ...	... e gitmek ne kadar sürer?
How long does the train stop?	Tren ne kadar (zaman) duruyor?
When would you like me to wake you up?	Saat kaçta uyandırmamı istiyorsunuz?
Please wake me up at seven in the morning!	Lütfen beni sabah saat yedide uyandırınız!
When does the postman come?	Postacı saat kaçta geliyor?
He usually comes at eight a.m.	Genellikle saat sekizde gelir.
How old are you?	Kaç yaşındasınız?
When is your next birthday?	Doğum gününüz ne zaman?
My birthday is on the 16 March.	Doğum günüm 16 Martta.
Please be punctual!	Lütfen zamanında geliniz!
Don't arrive at the last moment!	Son dakikada gelmeyiniz!

Telling the time

GEÇE   KALA   At one p.m.

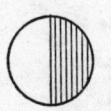

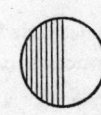

Saat birde	Saat biri on geçe. At ten past one.	Saat biri çeyrek geçe. At a quarter past one.	Saat bir buçukta. At half past one.

KEY TO PRONUNCIATION

c (jar), ç (church), g (gale), ğ (lengthen the preceding vowel), h (hill), ı (Cyril), j (Fr. *jeune*), ö (Fr. *peu* or Germ. *Köln*), s (sister), ş (shoe), ü (Fr. *dune* or Ger. *Glück*)

CEÇİYOR VAR

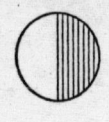

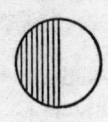

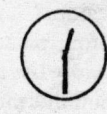

Saat yediyi on geçiyor.	Saat dokuza beş var.	On iki, Öğle, gece yarısı.	Yarım. Half past twelve.
It is ten past seven.	It is five to nine.	Noon, midnight, twelve o'clock.	

Phrases

What time is it?	Saat kaç?
It is late.	Geç oldu.
It is early yet.	Daha erken.
It is one o'clock, two, three ...	Saat bir, iki, üç ...
It is ten past one.	(Saat) biri on geçiyor.
It is a quarter past two.	(Saat) ikiyi çeyrek geçiyor.
It is half past five.	Saat beş buçuk.
It is twenty to seven.	(Saat) Yediye yirmi var.
It is quarter to eight.	Sekize çeyrek var.
It is noon.	Öğle, Saat on iki.
It is midnight.	Gece yarısı.
It is half past twelve.	Saat yarım.
When will you be coming?	Ne zaman geleceksin?
I shall be coming at ten a.m.	Sabah saat onda geleceğim.
What time is it now?	Şimdi saat kaç?
It is half past eleven.	Onbir buçuk.
At seven o'clock in the morning.	Sabah saat yedide.
At five o'clock in the evening.	Akşam saat beşte.
My watch is slow.	Saatim geri kalıyor.
My watch is fast.	Saatim ileri gidiyor.
You have plenty of time.	Daha çok vaktiniz var.

KEY TO PRONUNCIATION
c (jar), ç (church), g (gale), ğ (lengthen the preceding vowel), h (hill), ı (Cyril), j (Fr. *jeune*), ö (Fr. *peu* or Ger. *Köln*), s (sister), ş (shoe), ü (Fr. *dune* or Ger. Glück)

Time

I'm afraid it's time we left.	Korkarım, gitmek zamanı geldi.
Take your time.	Aceleye mahal yok.
I am in a hurry.	Acelem var!
Hurry up! Please!	Çabuk ol! Lütfen!
She has come early.	Erken geldi.
Why are you late?	Niçin geç kaldınız?
Where can she be?	Nerede olabilir?
	(Nerede kaldı?)
There she is!	İşte geldi!
How long does it take?	Ne kadar sürer?
It won't take more than two hours.	İki saatten fazla sürmez.
Will it take an hour to get there?	Oraya gitmek bir saat sürer mi?
My watch has stopped!	Saatim durmuş!
Will you please tell me the time?	Saati söyler misiniz, lütfen?

KEY TO PRONUNCIATION

c (jar), ç (church), g (gale), ğ (lengthen the preceding vowel), h (hill), ı (Cyril), j (Fr. *jeune*), ö (Fr. *peu* or Ger. *Köln*), s (sister), ş (shoe), ü (Fr. *dune* or Ger. *Glück*)

6 Weather and geographical expressions

Turkey lies between latitude 36° N and 42° N and longitude 26° E and 45° E and covers an area of 780,576 square kilometres (296,185 square miles). Of this 23,623 square kilometres are in Europe and the remainder, which is called Anatolia, is in Asia. Anatolia is an elongated rectangular extension of Asia lying between the Black Sea and the Mediterranean stretching as far as the Aegean and the Marmara seas. This solid plateau is a peninsula of 1,500 km. long and 600 km. wide with an average altitude of 1,100 metres. It is dominated by the Pontic ranges and the Black Sea mountains in the north, and by the Taurus mountains in the south.

Turkey has four different climates. The Mediterranean climate which prevails in the South and West has hot dry summers and mild wet winters. The Black Sea climate which affects the North has warm summers, mild winters and sufficient rainfall at all seasons. The continental climate is enjoyed in the North East with fairly warm summers, but very cold winters and sufficient rainfall at all seasons. The semi-arid climate prevails in the interior and South East, with cold winters and hot, dry summers. Thus, as Turkey contains all the climatic characteristics of the continent of Asia it was called Asia Minor by its ancient settlers.

Between May and October, Turkey is a country with sunshine practically all the time, the temperature is in the eighties and over.

Bounded by the Black, Marmara, Aegean and Mediterranean Seas, and the Straits of Bosphorus and the Dardanelles on its three sides, Turkey is completely surrounded by beautiful beaches. Very popular is the Turquoise Coast or the Turkish Riviera at Antalya which stretches for over three hundred miles. This sun-washed and orange-perfumed crescent from Kaş on the West to Anamur on the East is also called the Scimitar of Sand. The sea-bathing season in Antalya begins in April and continues until November.

In the tourism market, Turkey is advertised as having 300 days of

Weather and geographical expressions

sunshine a year, and is recommended as a tourist venue all the year round.

Vocabulary

English	Turkish	English	Turkish
Aegean	Ege	harbour	liman
air	hava	heat	sıcaklık
bay	koy	hot	sıcak
beach	kumsal, plaj	ice	buz
Black Sea	Karadeniz	island	ada
bolt	yıldırım	lake	göl
Bosphorus	Boğaziçi	land	toprak
breeze	meltem	light	ışık
canal	kanal	lighthouse	deniz feneri
cape	burun	lightning	şimşek
cave	mağara	log	kütük
city	şehir	lukewarm	ılık
climate	iklim	map	harita
cliff	uçurum	Marmora Sea	Marmara Denizi
cloud	bulut		
coast	sahil, kıyı	marsh	bataklık
cold	soğuk	Mediterranean	Akdeniz
country	memleket, vatan	mist	sis
countryside	kır, kırlık	mountain	dağ
dawn	şafak, gündoğuşu	moss	yosun
		north	kuzey
desert	çöl	north east	kuzey doğu
earthquake	deprem, zelzele	north west	kuzey batı
east	doğu	peninsula	yarımada
field	tarla	plain	ova
fog	sis	rain	yağmur
footpath	keçiyolu, patika	rainbow	gökkuşağı, eleğimsağma
forest	orman		
gale	kasırga	ravine	derin dere
gulf	körfez	river	nehir
hail	dolu	road	yol

KEY TO PRONUNCIATION

c (jar), ç (church), g (gale), ğ (lengthen the preceding vowel), h (hill), ı (Cyril), j (Fr. *jeune*), ö (Fr. *peu* or Ger. *Köln*), s (sister), ş (shoe), ü (Fr. *dune* or Ger. *Glück*)

Weather and geographical expressions

sea	deniz	temperature	ısı
shore	deniz kıyısı	thunder	gökgürültüsü
sky	gök	town	kasaba
snow	kar	valley	vadi
south	güney	warm	sıcak
south east	güney doğu	waterfall	çağlayan
south west	güney batı	weather	hava
spring	ilkbahar	west	batı
star	yıldız	wind	rüzgâr
stream	ırmak	wood	koru
storm	fırtına		

Phrases

What is the weather like?	Hava nasıl?
Is it likely to rain?	Yağmur yağacak mı?
It looks like rain.	Yağacağa benziyor.
It is lovely weather!	Nefis bir hava!
Do you think the weather will remain fine?	Hava böyle güzel kalacak mı dersiniz?
It is very hot.	Çok sıcak.
I cannot stand the heat!	Sıcağa dayanamıyorum!
The sky is overcast.	Hava kapalı.
Not a cloud in the sky!	Gökte tek bulut yok!
It is too sunny here, let's sit in the shade.	Burası çok güneşli, gölgede oturalım.
It is so peaceful.	O kadar sakin.
Is this a storm?	Bu fırtına mı?
I don't want to get wet.	Islanmak istemiyorum.
No, it is only a shower.	Hayır, sadece bir sağnak.
Is it going to be windy?	Hava rüzgârlı mı olacak?
Will the sea be rough, do you think?	Deniz dalgalı mı olacak dersiniz?
What did the weather forecast say?	Hava raporunda ne dedi?
Is the mountain pass blocked by snow?	Dağ geçidi karla kapalı mı?

KEY TO PRONUNCIATION

c (jar), ç (church), g (gale), ğ (lengthen the preceding vowel), h (hill), ı (Cyril), j (Fr. *jeune*), ö (Fr. *peu* or Ger. *Köln*), s (sister), ş (shoe), ü (Fr. *dune* or Ger. Glück)

Weather and geographical expressions

It is very slippery, be careful!	Yerler çok kaygan, dikkat ediniz!
What fine weather you have.	Havanız ne kadar güzel.
The sun is so warm and pleasant.	Güneş öyle ılık ve tatlı ki.
Will there be stars tonight?	Gece yıldızlı mı olacak?
I like sailing in moonlit waters.	Ayışıklı sularda sandalla gezmesini severim.
Are there waterfalls in Antalya?	Antalyada çağlıyanlar var mı?
What is the sea temperature?	Suyun ısı derecesi ne?
Is that a star or the light of a lighthouse?	O yıldız mı yoksa deniz feneri ışığı mı?
Is this a cloud or mountain mist?	Bu bulut mu yoksa dağ sisi mi?
After thunder and lightning, a beautiful rainbow!	Gök gürültüsü ve şimşeklerden sonra, güzel bir gökkuşağı!

KEY TO PRONUNCIATION

c (jar), ç (church), g (gale), ğ (lengthen the preceding vowel), h (hill), ı (Cyril), j (Fr. *jeune*), ö (Fr. *peu* or Ger. *Köln*), s (sister), ş (shoe), ü (Fr. *dune* or Ger. *Glück*)

7 Countries; nationalities; family and relationships

Continents	*Kıtalar*
Africa	Afrika
America	Amerika
Asia	Asya
Australia	Avustralya
Europe	Avrupa

Country		*Inhabitant*	
Afghanistan	Afganistan	Afghani	Afganlı
Albania	Arnavutluk	Albanian	Arnavut
Argentina	Arjantin	Argentinian	Arjantinli
Austria	Avusturya	Austrian	Avusturyalı
Belgium	Belçika	Belgian	Belçikalı
Brazil	Brezilya	Brazilian	Brezilyalı
Bulgaria	Bulgaristan	Bulgarian	Bulgar
Canada	Kanada	Canadian	Kanadalı
China	Çin	Chinese	Çinli
Cyprus	Kıbrıs	Cypriot	Kıbrıslı
Czechoslovakia	Çekoslovakya	Czech	Çekoslovakyalı
Denmark	Danimarka	Dane	Danimarkalı
England	İngiltere	Englishman	İngiliz
Ethiopia	Habeşistan	Ethiopian	Habeş
Finland	Finlanda	Finn	Finlandalı
France	Fransa	Frenchman	Fransız
Germany	Almanya	German	Alman
Ghana	Gana	Ghanaian	Ganalı

KEY TO PRONUNCIATION
c (jar), ç (church), g (gale), ğ (lengthen the preceding vowel), h (hill), ı (Cyril), j (Fr. *jeune*), ö (Fr. *peu* or Ger. *Köln*), s (sister), ş (shoe), ü (Fr. *dune* or Ger. Glück)

Countries; nationalities; family and relationships

Country		Inhabitant	
Greece	Yunanistan	Greek	Yunanlı
Holland	Holanda	Dutchman	Holandalı
Hungary	Macaristan	Hungarian	Macar
Iceland	İzlanda	Icelander	İzlandalı
India	Hindistan	Indian	Hintli
Ireland	İrlanda	Irishman	İrlandalı
Iran	İran	Iranian	İranlı
Iraq	Irak	Iraqi	Iraklı
Israel	İsrail	Israeli	İsrailli
Italy	İtalya	Italian	İtalyan
Japan	Japonya	Japanese	Japon
Jordan	Ürdün	Jordanian	Ürdünlü
Lebanon	Lübnan	Lebanese	Lübnanlı
Libya	Libya	Libyan	Libyalı
Mexico	Meksika	Mexican	Meksikalı
Morocco	Fas	Moroccan	Faslı
Netherlands	Holanda Felemenk	Dutchman	Holandalı Felemenk
New Zealand	Yeni Zelanda	New Zealander	Yeni Zelandalı
Norway	Norveç	Norwegian	Norveçli
Pakistan	Pakistan	Pakistani	Pakistanlı
Poland	Polonya Lehistan	Pole	Polonyalı, Leh
Portugal	Portekiz	Portuguese	Portekizli
Rumania	Romanya	Rumanian	Romanyalı
Russia	Rusya	Russian	Rus
Scotland	Iskoçya	Scot	Iskoçyalı
Spain	Ispanya	Spaniard	Ispanyol
South Africa	Güney Afrika	South African	Güney Afrikalı
Sweden	İsveç	Swede	İsveçli
Sudan	Sudan	Sudanese	Sudanlı
Switzerland	İsviçre	Swiss	İsviçreli
Syria	Suriye	Syrian	Suriyeli
Turkey	Türkiye	Turk	Türk

KEY TO PRONUNCIATION
c (jar), ç (church), g (gale), ğ (lengthen the preceding vowel), h (hill), ı (Cyril), j (Fr. *jeune*), ö (Fr. *peu* or Ger. *Köln*), s (sister), ş (shoe), ü (Fr. *dune* or Ger. *Glück*)

Countries; nationalities; family and relationships

Country		Inhabitant	
United Kingdom	Birleşik Kırallık	Briton	Britanyalı
U.S.A.	Amerika Birleşik Devletleri	American	Amerikalı
U.A.R.	Birleşik Arap Cumhuriyeti	Arab	Arap
U.S.S.R.	Sovyetler	Soviet Russian	Sovyet Rus
Wales	Galya	Welshman	Galyalı
Yugoslavia	Yugoslavya	Yugoslav	Yugoslav

Family and relationships

acquaintance	tanıdık, ahbap, dost
aunt (mother's sister)	teyze
aunt (father's sister)	hala
bride	gelin
bridegroom	güvey
brother	erkek kardeş, ağabey
brother-in-law (sister's husband)	enişte
brother-in-law (wife's brother)	kayınbirader
child	çocuk
cousin	kuzen, kuzin, teyzezade, halazade
daughter	kız (kız evlât)
daughter-in-law	gelin
family	aile, familya
father	baba
friend	arkadaş, dost
godfather	manevi baba, vaftiz babası
godmother	vaftiz anası
grandchild	torun
grandmother, grandma	nine, babaanne
grandfather, grandpa	dede, büyükbaba
grand-daughter	kız torun

KEY TO PRONUNCIATION

c (jar), ç (church), g (gale), ğ (lengthen the preceding vowel), h (hill), ı (Cyril), j (Fr. *jeune*), ö (Fr. *peu* or Ger. *Köln*), s (sister), ş (shoe), ü (Fr. *dune* or Ger. Glück)

Countries; nationalities; family and relationships

grandson	erkek torun
husband	koca, eş
mother	anne, ana
mother-in-law	kaynana, kayınvalde
nephew	yeğen
niece	yeğen
nurse	dadı
parents	ana baba, ebeveyn
relatives	akraba
son	oğul, erkek evlât
son-in-law	damat
sister	kızkardeş, abla
sister-in-law (husband's sister)	görümce
sister-in-law (wife's sister)	baldız
stepdaughter	üvey kız
stepfather	üvey baba
stepmother	üvey ana
uncle	amca, dayı
wife	karı, eş

Phrases

Where are you from?	Siz nerelisiniz?
What is your nationality?	Milliyetiniz nedir?
I am English.	Ben İngilizim.
I am Irish.	İrlandalıyım.
I am a Scotsman.	Iskoçyalıyım.
I am Welsh.	Galyalıyım.
I have an American passport.	Amerikan pasaportum var.
Are you a Turk?	Türk müsünüz?
From which country do you come?	Hangi memleketten geliyorsunuz?
What is your mother tongue?	Anadiliniz nedir?
Are you married?	Evli misiniz?
Where is your wife?	Karınız nerede? (Eşiniz nerede?)
Where does your husband work?	Kocanız nerede çalışıyor?
Have you got a family?	Çoluk çocuk var mı?

KEY TO PRONUNCIATION
c (jar), ç (church), g (gale), ğ (lengthen the preceding vowel), h (hill), ı (Cyril),
j (Fr. *jeune*), ö (Fr. *peu* or Ger. *Köln*), s (sister), ş (shoe), ü (Fr. *dune* or Ger. *Glück*)

I have a son and a daughter.	Bir oğlum ve bir kızım var.
How old is your son?	Oğlunuz kaç yaşında?
He is thirty-two.	Otuz iki yaşında.
Is he married?	Evli mi?
Yes, my daughter-in-law is German.	Evet, gelinim Almandır.
Have you any grandchildren?	Torununuz var mı?
No, I have no grandchildren.	Hayır, torunum yok.
Who is he? A relative of yours?	O kim? bir akrabanız mı?
No. He is just an acquaintance.	Hayır. Sadece bir tanıdık.
Is she your sister or your aunt?	Kızkardeşiniz mi, yoksa teyzeniz mi?
Is she a British subject?	Birkleşik Kırallık uyrukluğundan mı?
She is my cousin.	Kuzinimdir.
Is your father living?	Babanız hayatta mı?
He died ten years ago.	On yıl önce öldü.
It was a pleasure meeting your family.	Ailenizle tanışmak benim için zevk oldu.

KEY TO PRONUNCIATION

c (jar), ç (church), g (gale), ğ (lengthen the preceding vowel), h (hill), ı (Cyril), j (Fr. *jeune*), ö (Fr. *peu* or Germ. *Köln*), s (sister), ş (shoe), ü (Fr. *dune* or Ger. Glück)

8   Travel

Air travel

Istanbul is only three and a half jet hours from London and about ten flying hours from New York, and Turkey is served by almost all international airlines from the major cities of the world. Turkish Airlines (T.H.Y.) have flights from Amsterdam, Athens, Berlin, Brussels, Copenhagen, Frankfurt, Geneva, London, Milan, Munich, Rome, Stockholm, Vienna and Zurich, also operating all commercial passenger-carrying aircraft within the boundaries of Turkey. A network of daily flights throughout the country has been scheduled to include practically every airport that can accommodate the airline's Boeing 707, 727, 737 as well as DC 8, DC 9 and DC 10s. The safety record of T.H.Y. is one of the best in the world, and the service is swift, efficient and punctual. If one has a lot to see in a short time, it is well worth flying from one place to another.

T.H.Y. tickets carry a 10 per cent reduction for families on domestic flights, and children between the ages of 2 and 12 get 50 per cent reduction both on international and domestic flights. Members of the Press, school children and university students are all entitled to fare reductions. For more detailed information one should approach the Turkish Airlines Office in London at 11–12 Hannover Street, W1R 9HF.

Vocabulary

aeroplane, airplane	uçak	air-sickness	uçak tutması, hava tutması
air hostess	hostes	altitude	yükseklik, rakım
airline	havayolları, hava şirketi	apron	önlük, apron
airport	hava meydanı	cloud	bulut

KEY TO PRONUNCIATION
c (jar), ç (church), g (gale), ğ (lengthen the preceding vowel), h (hill), ı (Cyril), j (Fr. *jeune*), ö (Fr. *peu* or Ger. *Köln*), s (sister), ş (shoe), ü (Fr. *dune* or Ger. *Glück*)

control tower	kontrol kulesi	route	rota
cotton-wool	pamuk	runway	uçak havalanma pisti
crew	tayfa, mürettebat	seat	yer
extinguish, to	söndürmek	seat-belt	kemer
fasten, to	bağlamak	smoking	sigara içmek
fog	sis	steward	kamarot
jet aircraft	jet uçağı	tablet	tablet, hap
land, to	inmek	take off, to	havalanmak
landing	iniş	take off	havalanış
luncheon	öğle yemeği	tray	tepsi
paper bag	kâğıt torba	visibility	rüyet, görünürlük
passenger	yolcu		
pilot	pilot	window	pencere
propeller	pervane	wing	kanat
refreshments	yiyecek içecek şeyler		

Phrases

I want to fly to Istanbul. Can you make a booking for me?	Istanbula uçmak istiyorum. Bana yer kapatabilir misiniz?
When does the next plane leave for ...?	... 'a ilk uçak saat kaçta kalkıyor?
Are the flights fully booked?	Uçaklar dolu mu?
Do you think there is a chance of a cancellation?	Yeraçılma ihtimali var mı?
We are three, myself, my wife and my son.	Üç kişiyiz. Karım, oğlum ve ben.
The child is on my wife's passport.	Çocuk karımın pasaportuna kayıtlı.
May I see your passports, please.	Pasaportlarınıza bakabilir miyim, lütfen.
Here you are.	Buyrunuz.

KEY TO PRONUNCIATION
c (jar), ç (church), g (gale), ğ (lengthen the preceding vowel), h (hill), ı (Cyril), j (Fr. *jeune*), ö (Fr. *peu* or Ger. *Köln*), s (sister), ş (shoe), ü (Fr. *dune* or Ger. Glück)

Travel

How much money have you?	Ne kadar paranız var?
£50 in Traveller's Cheques and £15 in cash.	Elli sterlinlik tarvelers çek ve onbeş sterlin nakit para.
Do you have any Turkish liras?	Türk lirası var mı?
Yes. We have 100 Turkish liras.	Evet. Yüz Türk liramız var.
Which is your luggage?	Eşyalarınız hangileri?
It is over there.	Şu tarafta duruyor.
Please ask the porter to bring them here.	Hamala buraya getirmesini söyleyiniz lütfen.
Porter, bring that luggage here!	Hamal, şu eşyaları buraya getir!
That is not mine.	O benim değil.
I shall take this one myself.	Bunu ben kendim taşıyacağım.
Be very careful with this suitcase.	Bu bavula çok dikkat et.
Porter, do not leave this behind!	Hamalefendi, şunu arkada bırakma!
Bring them all here.	Hepisini buraya getir.
Have you anything to declare?	Deklare edecek bir şeyiniz var mı?
I have nothing to declare.	Deklare edecek bir şeyim yok.
Have you got any perfume, or alcohol?	Parfön veya alkol var mı?
No, there isn't any.	Hayır, yok.
What's in that suitcase?	O bavulda neler var?
Only our clothes.	Sadece giyecek eşyamız.
Have you had your money and valuables entered in your passport?	Para ve kıymetli eşyanızı pasaportunuza yazdırdınız mı?
Any gifts for friends?	Eşe dosta hediye var mı?
Anything valuable?	Kıymetli eşya?
This is all we have.	Hepsi bu kadar.
We are here only for a fortnight.	Sadece onbeş gün için geldik.
Have you any other luggage?	Başka eşyanız var mı?
I have a radio.	Bir radyom var.
— tape-recorder.	— teypim var.
— typewriter.	— daktilom var.
— transistor.	— transistör radyom var.

KEY TO PRONUNCIATION

c (jar), ç (church), g (gale), ğ (lengthen the preceding vowel), h (hill), ı (Cyril), j (Fr. *jeune*), ö (Fr. *peu* or Ger. *Köln*), s (sister), ş (shoe), ü (Fr. *dune* or Ger. *Glück*)

Travel

Where is your camera?	Fotoğraf makineniz nerede?
I have a cine-camera.	Bir sinema makinem var.
Has your luggage been examined?	Eşyalarınız muayene edildi mi?
Yes. This is already marked.	Evet. Buna işaret konuldu.
You have not marked this one.	Buna işaret koymadınız.
Is this all now?	Hepsi bu kadar mı?
Can we go now?	Şimdi gidebilir miyiz?
I have left my keys on the counter.	Anahtarlarımı masada bıraktım.
Shall I call you a porter?	Size bir hamal çağırayım mı?
We already have one.	Bir hamalımız var.
Have you booked your hotel?	Otelde yer ayırttınız mı?
You can use this telephone, if you like.	Bu telefonu kullanabilirsiniz, isterseniz.
Thank you for reminding us.	Hatırlatmanıza teşekkür ederim.
Have a nice time in our country!	Memleketimizde güzel eğleniniz!
I have a favour to ask of you.	Sizden bir recam var.
What is it?	Nedir?
Help me to close this case.	Bu çantayı kapatmama yardım ediniz.
I cannot find the porter.	Hamalı bulamıyorum.
How much do I owe you?	Ne kadar vereceğiz?
Whatever you like.	Ne isterseniz.
. . . lira for each piece.	Parçasına . . . lira
Find me a taxi or a dolmuş.*	Bana bir taksi veya dolmuş bul.
Please show me where the air line coach is.	Uçak otobüsünün nerede olduğunu lüften gösteriniz.
Is the plane late?	Uçak tehirli mi?
It is landing now.	Uçak iniyor, şimdi.
The plane is taking off.	Uçak havalanıyor.
Is there a plane for . . . today?	Bugün . . . 'ya uçak var mı?
What time does it take off?	Saat kaçta kalkıyor?

*Dolmuş – in Turkey, a 'shared taxi'. See under 'Coach Travel and the Dolmuş', p. 64.

KEY TO PRONUNCIATION

c (jar), ç (church), g (gale), ğ (lengthen the preceding vowel), h (hill), ı (Cyril), j (Fr. *jeune*), ö (Fr. *peu* or Ger. *Köln*), s (sister), ş (shoe), ü (Fr. *dune* or Ger. Glück)

Travel

When does it land at . . . ?	. . . ya ne zaman varıyor?
Does it stop anywhere *en route*?	Yolda başka yere iniş yapıyor mu?
I want to reserve a seat on the plane tomorrow leaving for . . .	Yarın . . . ya gidecek uçakta bir yer kapatmak istiyorum.
I do not feel well.	Kendimi iyi hissetmiyorum.
I think I am air-sick.	Galiba beni uçak tuttu.
Bring me some water, please.	Bana bir az su getiriniz.
— cotton-wool.	— pamuk.
— coffee.	— kahve.
What is that island called?	O adanın adı nedir?
We shall land at . . . in three minutes.	Üç dakikaya kadar . . . 'ye ineceğiz.
Extinguish your cigarettes!	Sigaralarınızı söndürünüz!
Fasten your seat-belts, please.	Kemerlerinizi bağlayınız, lütfen.
I cannot fasten my seat-belt.	Kemerimi bağlıyamıyorum.
Hostess, please give me my overcoat.	Hostes, lütfen bana paltomu veriniz.
Thank you, I don't need it.	Teşekkür ederim, ihtiyacım kalmadı.
Is this cloud or fog?	Bu bulut mu, yoksa sis mi?
How long does the flight last?	Uçuş ne kadar sürüyor?

Travel by rail

The cheapest way of getting to Turkey from England is by train and Istanbul is connected to almost all the most important cities of Europe by rail.

There is an express train every day crossing France, Switzerland and Italy, as well as the famous Orient Express which runs from London via Dover, Calais, Paris, Lausanne, Brigue, Milan to Venice. From Venice, there is a daily service for Istanbul by the 'Istanbul Express' via Trieste, Belgrade, Niş, Sofia, Svilengrad, Edirne to Istanbul.

There are also two daily services for Istanbul from Munich by the 'Istanbul Express' and the 'Tauern-Orient Express' via Salzburg, Zagreb, Belgrade and Sofia.

Another daily service for Istanbul departs from Vienna, the 'Balkan Express' which runs via Graz, Zagreb, Belgrade, Sofia, Svilengrad and Edirne to Istanbul.

KEY TO PRONUNCIATION

c (jar), ç (church), g (gale), ğ (lengthen the preceding vowel), h (hill), ı (Cyril), j(Fr. *jeune*), ö (Fr. *peu* or Ger. *Köln*), s (sister), ş (shoe), ü (Fr. *dune* or Ger. *Glück*)

Travel

The Turkish State Railway system maintains some 5,000 miles of excellent railroads, connecting even the most remote part of the country with the large cities. Two means of travel are provided by these railways – the night sleeper and the diesel day trains. On diesels there is one class only, second class; other trains usually have first, second and third classes.

The night sleepers accommodate one or two persons to a compartment. They are very comfortable and always have a dining car in which food and refreshment are provided. The diesel trains also have a snack bar where meals or refreshments are served to passengers.

There is a 20 per cent reduction on return tickets when travelling in Turkey. Students and members of the Press also enjoy reductions amounting to 50 per cent on trains, while groups of more than 15 enjoy 30 per cent reduction.

Vocabulary

back to the engine	arkası lokomotife, ters
blanket	battaniye
booking office	seyahat acentalığı, bilet gişesi
bookstall	kitap sergisi, kitapçı
bridge	köprü
carriage	vagon
change for	aktarma
cloakroom	gardrop
compartment	kompartıman
corridor	koridor
couchette	kuşet
diesel rail car	motörtren
dining car	vagon restoran, lokantalı vagon
door	kapı
engaged	meşgul, dolu
engine	lokomotif
enquiry	sorgu
entrance	giriş
exit	çıkış
facing the engine	lokomotif istikametinde, doğru
footboard	basamak
gate	dış kapı
guard	tren muhafaza memuru, bekçi, nöbetçi
journey	yolculuk
lean out, to	sarkmak, dışarı sarkmak
level-crossing	tren geçit kavşağı
luggage-van	furgon
passenger	yolcu
pillow	yastık
platform	peron
rack	parmaklıklı raf
rails	raylar
railway	demiryolu, tren
reduction	tenzilat, indirim

KEY TO PRONUNCIATION

c (jar), ç (church), g (gale), ğ (lengthen the preceding vowel), h (hill), ı (Cyril), j (Fr. *jeune*), ö (Fr. *peu* or Ger. *Köln*), s (sister), ş (shoe), ü (Fr. *dune* or Ger. *Glück*)

Travel

refreshment room	büfe	student reduction	öğrenci indirimi
return ticket	gidip gelme bilet	subway	yeraltı yolu
seat	yer	ticket	bilet
seat reservation	yer rezervasyonu	ticket collector	bilet memuru
single ticket	gidiş bileti	time-table	tren tarifesi
sleeping car	yataklı vagon	track	demiryolu hattı
slow train	adi katar	train	tren
smoking compartment	sigara içilebilen kompartıman	toilet	tuvalet, W.C., yüz numara, aptesane
soot	kurum	tunnel	tünel
station	istasyon	vacant	boş, serbes
station-master	istasyon müdürü	waiting-room	bekleme salonu
		window	pencere

Phrases

Where is the station?	İstasyon nerede?
Where is the left-luggage office?	Eşya emanet yeri nerede?
At what time does the train leave for...?	...e tren saat kaçta kalkıyor?
Where do I get a ticket?	Bilet nereden alınıyor?
Is the booking office open now?	Bilet gişesi şimdi açık mı?
Give me a railway time-table, please.	Lütfen bana bir demiryolu tarifesi veriniz.
What time does it arrive at...?	...e tren saat kaçta varıyor?
Does this go to...?	Bu tren...e gider mi?
Give me a ticket to...	Bana...için bir bilet veriniz.
I want a second-class ticket to Ankara.	Ankaraya ikinci mevki bir bilet istiyorum.
I want a return ticket to İzmir.	İzmire gidip gelme bilet istiyorum.
Will the train be late?	Tren tehirli mi?
I have two first-class sleeper seats reserved.	İki kişilik birinci mevki yataklı yerim var.

KEY TO PRONUNCIATION

c (jar), ç (church), g (gale), ğ (lengthen the preceding vowel), h (hill), ı (Cyril), j (Fr. *jeune*), ö (Fr. *peu* or Ger. *Köln*), s (sister), ş (shoe), ü (Fr. *dune* or Ger. *Glück*)

From which platform does the train leave?	Tren hangi perondan kalkıyor?
How much extra must you pay for a berth in the sleeper?	Yataklı vagonda bir yatak için ne kadar fazla para ödemek lazım?
I want a seat by the window.	Pencere kenarı yer istiyorum.
I want to sit facing the engine.	Trenin gidiş yönünde yer istiyorum.
Where is the waiting-room?	Bekleme salonu nerede?
Please help me up.	Lütfen binmeme yardım ediniz.
Please help me down.	Lütfen inmeme yardım ediniz.
Please pass me that case.	Lütfen şu bavulu bana uzatınız!
Will you please put the cases on the rack?	Lütfen bavulları rafa koyar mısınız?
Where is the conductor?	Kondüktör nerede?
I want another seat.	Başka bir yer istiyorum.
Is this seat taken?	Buranın sahibi var mı?
I should like to be near the restaurant-car.	Vagon restorana yakın bir yer reca ediyorum.
Is a first-class seat available?	Birincide boş yer var mı?
I am willing to pay the excess.	Farkını vermeğe razıyım.
May I see your ticket, please?	Biletinizi görebilir miyim, lütfen?
I must have left my ticket in the compartment.	Biletimi kompartmanda bırakmış olacağım.
Shall I go and bring it here?	Gidip bileti getireyim mi?
I have left my bag in the restaurant car.	Vagon restoranda çantamı bırakmışım.
— my gloves	— eldivenlerimi
— my glasses	— gözlüklerimi
— my papers	— gaztelerimi
May I open the window?	Pencereyi açabilir miyim?
May I close the window?	Pencereyi kapatabilir miyim?
Can you please help me to close this window?	Bu pencereyi kapamama lütfen yardım edebilir misiniz?
Do not lean out of the window!	Pencereden dışarı sarkmayınız!

KEY TO PRONUNCIATION

c (jar), ç (church), g (gale), ğ (lengthen the preceding vowel), h (hill), ı (Cyril), j (Fr. *jeune*), ö (Fr. *peu* or Ger. *Köln*), s (sister), ş (shoe), ü (Fr. *dune* or Ger. Glück)

Travel

Where is the restaurant-car?	Vagon restoran nerede?
It's usually in the middle of the train.	Çoğu zaman trenin ortasında olur.
What time do they begin to serve?	Saat kaçta yemek servisi başlar?
I want to have breakfast now.	Şimdi kahvaltı etmek istiyorum.
When do I have to pay?	Parasını ne zaman ödemem lazım?
Where are we now?	Şimdi neredeyiz?
Where is the toilet?	Tuvalet ne tarafta?
Do I change my train here?	Burada mı aktarma edeceğim?
Where do I change for ...?	... e gitmek için nerede aktarma yapacağım?
Is this the right train for ...?	... e giden tren bu mu?
How long does the train stop here?	Tren burada ne kadar durur?
Do I have time to buy a paper?	Gazete satın alacak kadar vaktim var mı?
From which platform does the train for Adana leave?	Adana treni hangi perondan kalkıyor?
I have left something in the train.	Trende bir şey unutmuşum.
Where did you leave it?	Nerde unuttunuz?
I must have left it in the toilet.	Tuvalette bırakmış olmalıyım.
Was it something valuable?	Kıymetli bir şey miydi?
I have left my brief-case on the rack.	Çantamı rafta bırakmışım.
Shall I go and collect it myself?	Kendim gidip alayım mı?
Would you rather send me the brief-case later?	Yoksa bana çantami sonra mı gönderirsiniz?
I should like to leave my luggage at the left luggage office.	Eşyalarımı Emanet'e bırakmak istiyorum.
How much shall I have to pay?	Kaç para ödemem lazım?
I am travelling second and here is my ticket.	İkinci mevki seyahat ediyorum ve işte biletim.
Here is your ticket for your luggage.	Eşyalarınız için emanet biletiniz.
Would you direct me to the booking-office?	Bana bilet gişesinin yerini gösterebilir misiniz?

KEY TO PRONUNCIATION

c (jar), ç (church), g (gale), ğ (lengthen the preceding vowel), h (hill), ı (Cyril), j (Fr. *jeune*), ö (Fr. *peu* or Germ. *Köln*), s (sister), ş (shoe), ü (Fr. *dune* or Ger. *Glück*)

Would you please tell me whether this ticket is valid?	Bu biletin geçerli olup olmadığını lütfen söyler misiniz?
I am sorry this ticket is no longer valid.	Bu bilet artık geçerli değil, maalesef.
One second class single for Adapazarı.	Adapazarına bir ikinci mevki gidiş.
First class return to Ankara!	Ankaraya birinci mevki gidip gelme!
Must I change for Adapazarı?	Adapazarı için aktarma lazım mı?
Has the train for Adapazarı gone?	Adapazarı treni gitti mi?
Is there another train this afternoon?	Öğleden sonra başka bir tren var mı?
Will I have to wait long?	Çok bekliyecek miyim?
Have you missed the train for Ankara?	Ankara trenini mi kaçırdınız?
No, it was the Adapazarı train.	Hayır, Adapazarı trenini?
This is the wrong train. It stops at all stations.	Bu yanlış tren. Bütün istasyonlara uğruyor.
Has the last train gone?	Son tren gitti mi?
Driver, take me to a nearby hotel.	Şoför efendi, beni bu civarda bir otele götürünüz!
I have an early train to catch tomorrow.	Yarın erkenden trene yetişmem lazım.

Cruising and yachting

The coastline of Turkey is not only renowned for its great scenic beauty and historic interest but it is also a paradise for the archaeologist, where he can lay his hands on the remains of some twelve civilizations. The Turkish Maritime Lines have regular services between the ports of the Black Sea, the Marmara, the Aegean and the Mediterranean. The ships are large, comfortable and furnish all services including food and entertainment. Although most trips are direct routes to and from the major ports, several schedules allow for leisurely meandering from harbour to harbour along the entire coast of Turkey. On these cruises, the ships remain for a day or more at each stop, allowing ample time

KEY TO PRONUNCIATION
c (jar), ç (church), g (gale), ğ (lengthen the preceding vowel), h (hill), ı (Cyril), j (Fr. *jeune*), ö (Fr. *peu* or Ger. *Köln*), s (sister), ş (shoe), ü (Fr. *dune* or Ger. Glück)

Travel

for sightseeing and shopping ashore before going on to the next port. Swimming and skin-diving are also popular at some of these ports.

Tourists travelling to Turkey from abroad in their cars can board the Turkish Maritime Lines' ferryboat from Ancona during the months of May–October, and arrive at Izmir. There is also a ferryboat line sailing between Famagusta in Cyprus and Mersin in Turkey.

For family reductions and for special fares for journalists, teachers, students and diplomats, one should contact either the Turkish Tourism Information Office in your area or the representative of the Turkish Maritime Lines, Walford Lines Ltd, St Mary Axe House, London EC3A 8BB.

Vocabulary

aft	kıçta, kıça doğru	block	makara
aground	karaya oturmuş	boat	gemi, kayık, sandal
air mattress	içi havayla doldurulmuş şilte	bow	baş, pruva
alongside	bordasında, bordasına	bridge	köprü
		buoy	şamandıra, duba
anchor	demir, çapa	cabin	kamara
anchor, to	demirlemek	caique	kayık
bait	yem, olta yemi	captain	kaptan
bathe	yıkanmak, denize girmek	canoe	sandal
		chain	demir, zincir
bathing-cap	yüzme başlığı	coast	sahil
bathing-costume	mayo	crane	vinç
		crew	tayfa
bathing hut	soyunma yeri, kabin	crew-list	tayfa listesi
		current	akıntı, cereyan
bay	koy	Customs	Gümrük
beach	kumsal, plaj	deck	güverte
below	Aşağı, alt güverte	deck-chair	şezlong
berth	kamarada yatacak yer, palamar yeri	diesel fuel	mazot
		dinghy	şarpi, küçük kotra
bilge	sintine	dining-room	yemek salonu

KEY TO PRONUNCIATION

c (jar), ç (church), g (gale), ğ (lengthen the preceding vowel), h (hill), ı (Cyril), j (Fr. *jeune*), ö (Fr. *peu* or Ger. *Köln*), s (sister), ş (shoe), ü (Fr. *dune* or Ger. *Glück*)

disembark, to	gemiden karaya çıkmak	lifeboat	cankurtaran sandal
diving-board	atlama tahtası	lighthouse	deniz feneri
embark, to	gemiye binmek	lights	ışıklar
engine	makine, motör	mast	direk
engine-room	makine dairesi	mole	dalgakıran, mendirek
excursion	gezinti		
first class	birinci mevki	moor, to	demirde yatmak, şamandıraya bağlamak
fish, to	balık tutmak		
fishing-line	olta		
flippers	yüzmek için kullanılan takma el ve ayak, fliper	moorings	gemi bağlamağa mahsus palamar, yer
forward	ileri	motorboat	motörbot, deniz motörü
funnel	baca		
gangway	iskele tahtası, pasaj, yol	net	ağ
		paraffin	parafin
goggles	su gözlüğü	pebble	çakıl taşı
harbour	liman	plank	borda tahtası
harbour authorities	liman idaresi	port	liman, lumbar, geminin sol veya iskele tarafı
harpoon gun	zıpkın atan tüfek		
hatch	ambar ağzı, ambar kapağı	porthole	gemi penceresi, lumbar
hatch cover	ambar örtüsü	propeller	pervane, uskur
hold	gemi ambarı	purser	gemi veznedarı
hook	kanca, çengel	quay	rıhtım, iskele
hull	tekne	raft	sal
keel	gemi omurgası, omurga	rock	kaya
		rubber ring	lastik baba
island	ada	rudder	dümen
jelly-fish	denizanası	sail	yelken
lake	göl	sailor	gemici
lifebelt	cankurtaran kemeri	sand	kum, kumsal
		sand-dune	kum tepeleri

KEY TO PRONUNCIATION

c (jar), ç (church), g (gale), ğ (lengthen the preceding vowel), h (hill), ı (Cyril), j (Fr. *jeune*), ö (Fr. *peu* or Ger. *Köln*), s (sister), ş (shoe), ü (Fr. *dune* or Ger. Glück)

Travel

sea	deniz	sunstroke	güneş çarpması
sea-urchin	deniz böceği	swim, to	yüzmek
seasickness	deniz tutması	swimming-pool	yüzme havuzu
seashore	deniz kıyısı		
seaside	deniz kenarı	tiller	dümen yekesi
seaweed	deniz yosunu	tug, to	kuvvetle çekmek
shade	gölge, siper yer	tugboat	romorkör
shark	köpek balığı	towel	havlu
shallow	sığ	Tourist	turist
shell	deniz hayvanı kabuğu	Tourist Class	Turist sınıfı
		wave	dalga
shingle	çakıllı deniz kenarı	warp	palamar
		weather-forecast	hava raporu, hava tahmini
shore	kıyı		
shower	duş	wheel	çark, dümen dolabı, tekerlek
ship	gemi, vapur		
slipway	gemi yapı kızağı	wharf	yük iskelesi, antrepo
smoke	duman		
stern	geminin kıçı	winch	vinç
steward	kamarot	wind	rüzgâr, yel
sun	güneş	wire-rope	demir halat
sunshade	tente	wreck	geminin kazaya uğraması
submerge, to	suya batırmak		
submarine	denizaltı	yacht	yat

Phrases

Have you booked a cabin? — Kamaranızı kapattınız mı?
Direct me to the booking office, please. — Lütfen bana vapur bilet gişesini gösterir misiniz?
When are you sailing? — Ne zaman yola çıkacaksınız?
Is there a ship on Friday to Marmara Adası? — Marmara adasına, Cumaya vapur var mı?
Is there one on Sunday? — Pazara var mı?

KEY TO PRONUNCIATION

c (jar), ç (church), g (gale), ğ (lengthen the preceding vowel), h (hill), ı (Cyril), j (Fr. *jeune*), ö (Fr. *peu* or Ger. *Köln*), s (sister), ş (shoe), ü (Fr. *dune* or Ger. Glück)

What time does it sail?	Saat kaçta hareket ediyor?
How many knots does she do?	Kaç mil sürat yapıyor?
How long does the journey take?	Yolculuk ne kadar sürüyor?
I should like to visit the Black Sea coast.	Karadeniz sahilini gezmek istiyorum.
Is the Black Sea rough?	Karadeniz sert olur mu?
I want to see the Turkish Riviera.	Türk Rivyerasını görmek istiyorum.
Is there a regular service?	Devamlı bir servis var mı?
Please book me three places in the first class.	Lütfen bana üç kişilik birinci mevki bir kamara ayırınız!
I don't want to share the cabin, I want it for my family.	Kamarayı paylaşmak istemiyorum, ailem için bir kamara istiyorum.
How many berths are there in a cabin?	Bir kamarada kaç yatak var?
Does the price include meals?	Fiata yemekler dahil mi?
Isn't there a reduction for professors and students?	Profesörler ve öğrenciler için bir tenzilat yok mu?
I don't want to travel deck class.	Güvertede gitmek istemiyorum.
Can't I benefit from any reductions?	Hiç bir tenzilattan faydalanamaz mıyım?
I should like to book my return passage now.	Dönüş biletimi şimdiden almak istiyorum.
Would you tell me the name of the ship?	Geminin adını söyler misiniz?
Where does she stop on the voyage?	Yolda nerelerde duruyor?
Where does it sail from?	Nereden hareket ediyor?
I want to take my car with me.	Otomobilimi de birlikte götürmek istiyorum.
How much does it cost to take a car from Istanbul to İzmir?	İstanbüldan İzmire bir otomobil kaç paraya gidiyor?
Where is my cabin?	Kamaram nerede?
Where can I get a deck-chair?	Nereden şezlong alabilirim?
Is this the Purser's office?	Kamarotun ofisi burası mı?

KEY TO PRONUNCIATION

c (jar), ç (church), g (gale), ğ (lengthen the preceding vowel), h (hill), ı (Cyril), j (Fr. *jeune*), ö (Fr. *peu* or Ger. *Köln*), s (sister), ş (shoe), ü (Fr. *dune* or Ger. Glück)

Travel

Can I change my cabin, please?	Kamaramı değiştirebilir miyim?
I cannot stand the noise of the propellers.	Uskurun gürültüsüne dayanamıyorum.
This cabin is near the engine, and it is too hot.	Bu kamara makine dairesine yakın ve çok sıcak oluyor.
Where is the bathroom?	Banyo nerede?
Where is the shower?	Duş nerede?
Where can I send a wireless telegram?	Nereden bir tel gönderebilirim?
Is there a doctor on board?	Gemide bir doktor var mı?
My son has been seasick.	Oğlumu deniz tuttu.
Does the ship call at Bodrum?	Gemi Bodruma uğruyor mu?
How long does it stay?	Ne kadar kalıyor?
Can one go ashore?	Karaya çıkılabilir mi?
Doesn't the ship enter the harbour?	Gemi limana girmiyor mu?
No. One disembarks in small boats.	Hayır. Küçük kayıklarla çıkılıyor.
It is getting foggy.	Sis basıyor.
Get your passports ready.	Pasaportlarınızı hazırlayın!
The coast is in sight.	Sahil göründü.
Will you please show me the gangway?	Lütfen, karaya çıkış hangi taraftan, gösterebilir misiniz?
Where is the shipping agent's office?	Gemi Acentasının Bürosu nerede?
I should like to take the ferry from Izmir to Venice.	İzmirden Venediğe giden feribota binmek istiyorum.
Take me to the Harbour Master's Office!	Lütfen beni Liman Reisinin Bürosuna götürünüz!
Where did you come from?	Nereden geldiniz?
Where have you last anchored?	En son nerede demirlediniz?
How long are you staying?	Ne kadar kalacaksınız?
Where is the crew list?	Tayfa listesi nerede?
Is anyone ill?	İçinizde hasta olan var mı?
Where can I get stores?	Komanya (erzak) nereden alabilirim?

KEY TO PRONUNCIATION

c (jar), ç (church), g (gale), ğ (lengthen the preceding vowel), h (hill), ı (Cyril), j (Fr. *jeune*), ö (Fr. *peu* or Ger. *Köln*), s (sister), ş (shoe), ü (Fr. *dune* or Ger. Glück)

Can one get duty-free fuel?	Gümrük resimsiz mazot satın alınabilir mi?
I want water pumped aboard.	Pompayla su almak istiyorum.
Is the water deep enough for us?	Su derinliği bizim için yeter mi?
Isn't it too shallow?	Çok sığ değil mi?
Can I come alongside?	Bordanıza yanaşabilir miyim?
Can I anchor here?	Burada demirliyebilir miyim?
How much do you charge for water?	Suya kaç para alıyorsunuz?
— fuel?	Mazota kaç para alıyorsunuz?
Is there a strong current here?	Burada akıntı kuvvetli mi?
Is there a tide here?	Burada meddücezir (gelgit) olur mur?
There is no tide in Turkish waters.	Türk sularında meddücezir yoktur.

Coach travel and the 'Dolmuş'

A large number of coach lines has sprung up in Turkey during recent years, offering passenger comfort and safety comparable to any similar service in Europe, particularly between the major Turkish cities. These coaches are spacious, comfortable and operate on a strict time-table. The coach companies ask a fraction of the fares charged for train or plane travel, and some even supply food and refreshments while *en route*.

Most coaches are imported from Europe and many are plush with plastic domes and windows which allow an unobstructed view of the passing countryside. It is, however, recommended to secure a direct or 'ekspres' coach that makes no stops along the way. Local buses have a habit of stopping numerous times to let passengers on or off, resulting in late arrival at one's destination.

Dolmuş is a Turkish word which is applied by extension to the 'shared taxi'. Instead of hiring a taxi and paying the full fare, each passenger hires one of the five or eight seats in a motor-car and pays one-fifth or one-eighth of the fare, usually a fixed charge for a definite distance. This Dolmuş system was first introduced to solve the traffic problem in Istanbul and subsequently it spread to become the typical

KEY TO PRONUNCIATION
c (jar), ç (church), g (gale), ğ (lengthen the preceding vowel), h (hill), ı (Cyril), j (Fr. *jeune*), ö (Fr. *peu* or Ger. *Köln*), s (sister), ş (shoe), ü (Fr. *dune* or Ger. Glück)

Travel

Turkish form of transportation. One can find a Dolmuş to travel from one city or town to another at almost any time of the day. Although a bit more expensive, it is quicker and more comfortable than the coach or bus. Dolmuş cars usually have a yellow strip around the chassis and some carry lighted signs on the roof of the car showing the destination or the route of the Dolmuş.

Vocabulary

back seat	arkada oturacak yer	passenger	yolcu
bus	otobüs	radio	radyo
bus-stop	otobüs durağı	roof	çatı, dam
coach	otobüs	shared-taxi	dolmuş
coach-stop	otobüs durağı	stop, to	durmak
conductor	kondüktör, biletçi	suitcase	çanta
		taxi	taksi
dual carriage-way	çift yol	taxi rank	taksi (bekleme) durağı
		ticket	bilet
driver	şöför	transistor radio	transistörlü radyo
dusty	tozlu		
fare	yol parası	trolley-bus	troleybüs
front-seat	önde oturacak yer, önyer	underground-train	tünel
highway	karayolu, şose	window	pencere
inside	içersi	window seat	pencere kenarı yer
Inspector	kontrolör		
luggage	bavul	W.C.	tuvalet, yüz numara
one way	tek yön		

Phrases

I want to take a bus to Ankara.   Ankaraya otobüsle gitmek istiyorum.

Where can one find a bus for Ankara?   Ankaraya otobüs nereden kalkıyor?

KEY TO PRONUNCIATION

c (jar), ç (church), g (gale), ğ (lengthen the preceding vowel), h (hill), ı (Cyril), j (Fr. *jeune*), ö (Fr. *peu* or Ger. *Köln*), s (sister), ş (shoe), ü (Fr. *dune* or Ger. *Glück*)

Where can I find a shared taxi for İzmir?	İzmir dolmuşunu nerede bulabilirim?
Does this bus go to ...	Bu otobüs ... e gider mi?
Is this the stop for ...?	... için durak burası mı?
Is this a dolmuş car?	Bu otomobil dolmuş mu yapıyor?
Is this a dolmuş stop?	Burası dolmuş durağı mı?
Have you a spare wheel with you?	Yedek tekerlek (stepne) var mı?
Have you any spare parts with you?	Hiç yedek parçan var mı?
I want to get off at Bolu.	Bolu'da inmek istiyorum.
Do you go near Abant Lake?	Abant gölünün yakınından geçer mi?
Do you pass ...?	... dan geçer mi?
Drop me at the next stop.	Bu durakta ineceğim!
Call me a taxi please.	Lütfen bir taksi çağırınız.
Take me for a quick look round the town.	Şehri şöyle bir dolaşalım.
Show us round the principal monuments.	Ana anıtları gösteriniz.
Step on the gas! We don't have much time!	Gaza bas! Vaktimiz dar!
The traffic police took our number.	Polis numaramızı aldı.
Slow down, we want to stop here.	Yavaşla, burada durmak istiyoruz.
Please wait for a few minutes.	Lütfen bir kaç dakika bekleyiniz.
Can you put this suitcase beside you?	Bu çantayı yanına yerleştirebilir misin?
Can't we have our lunch at Abant?	Öğle yemeğimizi Abant'ta yiyemez miyiz?
Where do you stop for lunch?	Öğle yemeği için nerede duruyorsun?
How long does it take from Istanbul to Izmir by bus?	Otobüsle İstanbuldan İzmire ne kadar sürer?
Take us to the Topkapı Palace.	Bizi Topkapı Sarayına götür.

KEY TO PRONUNCIATION

c (jar), ç (church), g (gale), ğ (lengthen the preceding vowel), h (hill), ı (Cyril), j (Fr. *jeune*), ö (Fr. *peu* or Ger. *Köln*), s (sister), ş (shoe), ü (Fr. *dune* or Ger. Glück)

Travel

How much do you charge for the whole day?	Bütün günlüğüne kaç para istiyorsun?
How much do you charge for the half day?	Yarım gün için kaç para?
How much do you charge per Km.?	Kilometresi kaça?

KEY TO PRONUNCIATION

c (jar), ç (church), g (gale), ğ (lengthen the preceding vowel), h (hill), ı (Cyril), j (Fr. *jeune*), ö (Fr. *peu* or Ger. *Köln*), s (sister), ş (shoe), ü (Fr. *dune* or Ger. Glück)

9 Motoring

Motoring

Turkey may be reached by car either via Belgium, Germany, Austria, Yugoslavia and Bulgaria or by means of a regular drive-on drive-off ferry service from Ancona. The distance is 1,885 road miles from London to the magic city of Istanbul. It will take a motorist four to six days along the modern fast motorways. One could drive through France, Germany, Austria, Yugoslavia and Bulgaria, i.e. Calais-Köln (262 m), Köln-Nürnberg (256 m), Nürnberg-Munich (106 m), Munich-Zagreb (395 m), Zagreb-Belgrade (242 m), Belgrade-Sofia (244 m) and Sofia-Istanbul (380 m) or drive through Munich-Vienna (278 m), Vienna-Budapest (155 m), Budapest-Belgrade (240 m), the second alternative taking you an extra 36 miles.

Turkey has a network of modern roads which are gradually being extended and converted to bitumen. The highways linking cities are well-surfaced asphalt roads and traffic is not very heavy. The road through to Iran, via Ankara and Erzurum is mainly good, but poor near the frontier; the road over the Taurus Mountains to Syria via the Cilician Gates, is good throughout. Elsewhere the roads are reasonably good for sightseeing, except in the remote south-eastern part of the country.

Petrol in Turkey costs much less than it does in the UK and there are petrol stations (B.P., Shell, Mobil, Türk Petrol) practically everywhere at intervals of 10 miles. Service facilities in the towns and cities are good and inexpensive. Oil changes and complete servicing cost about half of what they do in Britain. A higher grade petrol (app. 94 octane) is now available at most filling stations on main highways.

In Turkey driving is on the right, overtaking on the left. Speed limits are 50 kph (30 mph) in built-up areas for all vehicles. In open country it is 90 kph (55 mph) for private cars, 80 kph (50 mph) for mini-buses, station wagons, vans; 70 kph (43 mph) for motor-cycles and lorries.

Headlights as well as sidelights must be used when driving after

Motoring

sunset or in poor visibility. When driving in congested city areas, dipped headlights should be used at all times. It is forbidden to overtake while constantly flashing the headlights or when using sidelights only. One must warn the driver of the vehicle concerned before overtaking. It is strictly forbidden to use horns in populated areas.

International road signs are used, and written signs are easy to understand. DUR means Stop, GEÇ means Cross. TEK YÖN means One Way, PARK YAPILMAZ means No Parking. TAŞIT GIREMEZ means No Entry for vehicles.

A visiting motorist is expected to have an international driving licence and must have an evidence of cover – a Green Card endorsed for Turkey. These can be obtained from the AA or the RAC. As third party insurance is compulsory in Turkey, the motorist should take out third party insurance at any of the insurance companies at the frontier posts when entering Turkey.

Visiting motorists can import their own vehicles free for a period of three months, including caravans and luggage trailers, hire cars and pleasure craft.

In case of an accident, the police should be informed and a police report of the accident taken. On the basis of this report your claim will be considered by the insurance company. The insurance company's agent should be informed and a photocopy of the police report should be handed over to him. Assistance and advice can be had from the Touring Automobile Club of Turkey, 364 Halâskâr Gazi Caddesi, Şişli Meydanı, Şişli, Istanbul.

Vocabulary

General

accident	kaza	driver	şoför
bus	otobüs	driving licence	şoför ehliyeti
car	otomobil	fine	para cezası
caravan	karavan	garage	garaj
collision	çarpışma	insurance	sigorta
distilled water	distile su	lorry	kamyon
to drive	otomobil kul- lanmak, sürmek	lubrication mechanic	yağlama usta

KEY TO PRONUNCIATION

c (jar), ç (church), g (gale), ğ (lengthen the preceding vowel), h (hill), ı (Cyril), j (Fr. *jeune*), ö (Fr. *peu* or Ger. *Köln*), s (sister), ş (shoe), ü (Fr. *dune* or Ger. Glück)

Motoring

motor-coach	otobüs	pump	pompa
motor-cycle	motosiklet	speed	hız, sürat
number-plate	plaka	traffic	trafik
oil	yağ	traffic-lights	trafik ışıkları
pedestrian	yaya	vehicle	taşıt
petrol	benzin		

The Chassis

axle	dingil	radiator	radyatör
brake	fren	shock absorber	amortisör
car tyre	lastik	spring, spring	yay, yay
differential	difransiyel	leaf	yaprağı
drive shaft	transmisyon şaftı	steering wheel	direksiyon volanı
drum	kasnak	wheel	tekerlek
petrol tank	benzin deposu		

The Engine

accelerator	gaz pedalı	fan	vantilatör
air filter	hava süzgeci	fan belt	vantilatör kayışı
battery	batarya, akümülatör, akü	gear box	vites kutusu
		gear lever	vites kolu
camshaft	mil dirseği şaftı	oil pump	yağ pompası
clutch	debriyaj	oil filter	yağ filtresi
clutch pedal	debriyaj pedalı	petrol pump	benzin pompası
carburettor	karbüretör	piston	piston
crankshaft	krank şaft	piston rings	piston segmanları
cylinder	silindir		
distributor	distribütör	sparking plug	buji
exhaust pipe	egzos borusu	valve spring	supap yayı
exhaust valve	egzos valvı		

Electrical parts

bulbs	ampuller	ignition	ateşleme
contact breaker	kontak tıpası	oil pressure gauge	yağ monometresi
dynamo	dinamo		

KEY TO PRONUNCIATION

c (jar), ç (church), g (gale), ğ (lengthen the preceding vowel), h (hill), ı (Cyril), j (Fr. *jeune*), ö (Fr. *peu* or Ger. *Köln*), s (sister), ş (shoe), ü (Fr. *dune* or Ger. Glück)

Motoring

petrol gauge	benzin monometresi	self-starter	marş, hareket teribatı
rotor arm	rotor kolu	speedometer	sürat ölçeği

The Car

boot	bagaj yeri	headlamps	farlar
bumper	tampon	bonnet	ön kapak
car windows	yan pencereler	mudguards	çamurluk
direction indicator	yön işareti	number plate	plaka
		rear light	arka ışık
door handle	kapı kolu	windscreen	ön cam
horn	klakson	windscreen wiper	cam sileceği
mirror	ayna, dikiz aynası	side lights	yan ışıklar
driver's seat	şöför mahalli		

Tools

file	eğe	screwdriver	tornavida
grease gun	yağlama tabancası	socket wrench	duy anahtar
		spanners	İngiliz anahtarı
hammer	çekiç	tyre levers	leviye
jack	kriko	tyre pump	lastik pompası
pliers	kerpeten		

Complaints at service stations

What is the matter with your car?	Otomobilinize ne oldu?
My car has broken down.	Otomobilim bozuldu.
There is something wrong with the engine.	Motörde bozukluk var.
There is something wrong with the dynamo.	Dinamoda bozukluk var.
There is something wrong with the lights.	Işıklar bozuk.
The brakes do not function properly.	Frenler iyi işlemiyor.

KEY TO PRONUNCIATION
c (jar), ç (church), g (gale), ğ (lengthen the preceding vowel), h (hill), ı (Cyril), j (Fr. *jeune*), ö (Fr. *peu* or Ger. *Köln*), s (sister), ş (shoe), ü (Fr. *dune* or Ger. Glück)

Something is wrong with the clutch.	Debriyaj bozuk.
My car won't start.	Motör çalışmıyor.
The self-starter doesn't work.	Kontakt çalışmıyor.
I have a puncture.	Lastik patladı.
The fuses are blown.	Sigortalar patlamış.
The radiator is leaking.	Radyatör akıyor.
The battery is not charging.	Akü (Batarya) şarj etmiyor.
The carburettor is choked.	Karbüretör tıkanmış.
I have run out of petrol.	Benzinim bitmiş.
This does not function properly.	Bu iyi işlemiyor.
There is a dent here.	Burada bir çöküntü var.
This needs straightening.	Bunun düzletilmesi lazım.
The wiper doesn't work.	Cam silecek çalışmıyor.
This must be replaced.	Bunun değiştirilmesi lazım.
The clutch needs relining.	Debriyaj ayarı lazım.
The battery needs recharging.	Akünün yeniden şarjedilmesi lazım.
The engine knocks.	Motör tekliyor.
The sparking plugs need cleaning.	Bujilerin temizlenmesi lazım.
I have blown a cylinder gasket.	Silindir jontası patlamış.
The front wheels need adjusting.	Ön tekerleklerin ayarlanması lazım.
The tappets require adjusting.	Supap ayarı lazım.
The car needs greasing and oiling.	Yağlama ve yağ değiştirme lazım.

Requests at garages

Can you tow the car?	Otomobili çekebilir misiniz?
Can you repair it?	Tamir edebilir misiniz?
Can you do it at once?	Hemen yapabilir misiniz?
Do you do repairs?	Tamir yapar mısınız?
Can you beat the dent out?	Bu çöküntüyü düzletebilir misiniz?
I want some water.	Su istiyorum.

KEY TO PRONUNCIATION

c (jar), ç (church), g (gale), ğ (lengthen the preceding vowel), h (hill), ı (Cyril), j (Fr. *jeune*), ö (Fr. *peu* or Ger. *Köln*), s (sister), ş (shoe), ü (Fr. *dune* or Ger. Glück)

Motoring

I want some petrol.	Benzin istiyorum.
I want four gallons.	Dört galon benzin istiyorum.
Please, fill her up.	Lütfen, tankı doldurunuz.
I want some motor oil.	Motör yağı istiyorum.
I want some brake oil.	Fren yağı istiyorum.
I want an inner tube.	Bir iç lastik istiyorum.
I want a new tyre.	Bir yeni lastik istiyorum.
I want a sparking plug.	Buji istiyorum.
I want some new bulbs.	Yeni ampul istiyorum.
I want garage space for the day.	Arabamı gündüz bırakacak yer istiyorum.
— for the night.	— gece için.
Will you adjust the brakes?	Frenleri ayarlar mısınız?
Will you repair this puncture?	Lastiği tamir eder misiniz?
Please fill the radiator.	Lütfen radyatörü doldurunuz.
Please clean the headlights.	Lütfen farları temizleyiniz.
Please show me how the gear works.	Lütfen vitesin nasıl işlediğini gösteriniz.
Please check the oil.	Lütfen yağı kontrol ediniz.
Please top the battery with distilled water.	Lütfen aküye distile su doldurunuz.
Please change this wheel.	Lütfen bu tekerleği değiştiriniz.
Please start the engine.	Lütfen motörü işletiniz.
Please wash the car.	Lütfen otomobili yıkayınız.
Please test the tyre pressures.	Lütfen lastik tazyikini ölçünüz.
Please take me to the owner of the garage.	Lütfen beni garajın sahibine götürünüz.
May I have the bill in detail, please?	Lütfen faturada hesabı dökümlü olarak gösterebilir misiniz?

Questions and directions

Can you help me?	Bana yardım edebilir misiniz?
Is there a hospital nearby?	Yakında hastane var mı?
What is the name of this village?	Bu köyün adı nedir?

KEY TO PRONUNCIATION
c (jar), ç (church), g (gale), ğ (lengthen the preceding vowel), h (hill), ı (Cyril), j (Fr. *jeune*), ö (Fr. *peu* or Ger. *Köln*), s (sister), ş (shoe), ü (Fr. *dune* or Ger. *Glück*)

Motoring

Can you show me on this map?	Bu hartada gösterir misiniz?
What time does the garage close?	Garaj saat kaçta kapanıyor?
Is the garage open all night?	Garaj bütün gece açık mı?
I want to leave early in the morning.	Sabah erkenden yola çıkmak istiyorum.
How long will it take to repair it?	Tamir ne kadar sürer?
What will the repairs cost?	Tamir kaça çıkacak?
Isn't it a bit expensive?	Biraz pahalı değil mi?
When will the car be ready?	Otomobil ne zaman hazır olacak?
Will it be ready this afternoon?	Öğleden sonraya hazır olur mu?
I will come for the car at six.	Saat altıda almağa gelirim.
I want to have a receipt.	Bir makbuz reca ediyorum.
You have not given me the correct change.	Paranın üstünü tamam vermediniz.
Will you please show me the road to ...?	Lütfen bana ... 'ya giden yolu gösterir misiniz?
Which way?	Ne taraftan?
Go straight on.	Dümdüz gidiniz.
Turn to the right.	Sağa dönünüz.
Turn to the left.	Sola dönünüz.
Take the first turning.	İlk yoldan sapınız.
Take the second turning on the left.	Soldaki ikinci yoldan sapınız.
Go back.	Geri gidiniz.
Stop at the traffic lights.	Trafik ışıklarında durunuz.
Go over the bridge.	Köprünün üstünden geçiniz.
— under.	— altından.
How long does it take to go to the frontier?	Sınıra gitmek ne kadar sürer?
How far off is the telephone?	Telefon ne kadar uzaktadır?
Can you show me the way to the first garage?	En yakın garaja giden yolu bana gösterir misiniz?
Can you come with me to show me the way?	Yolu göstermek için benimle gelebilir misiniz?

KEY TO PRONUNCIATION

c (jar), ç (church), g (gale), ğ (lengthen the preceding vowel), h (hill), ı (Cyril), j (Fr. *jeune*), ö (Fr. *peu* or Ger. *Köln*), s (sister), ş (shoe), ü (Fr. *dune* or Ger. Glück)

10 Camping, caravanning and cycling

Turkey has camping sites near all popular tourist attractions. The main sites in and near Istanbul are very popular. The Istanbul Municipality has several sites in Florya and the Timlo Company has a camp site at Ataköy with beautiful sandy beaches. Among the most developed sites are the BP Mocamps, linking tourist cities to one another. The BP Mocamp at Kartaltepe, which lies on the E5 Highway, has a swimming pool, shops, exchange office and an information centre. Information on facilities and rates per night at Kervansaray, Mocamps (BP) and other camping sites are available at Turkish Tourism Information Bureaux in the form of leaflets or brochures. In Bursa, Uludağ enjoys great popularity among campers. In summer the gay, colourful coasts around Marmara, Gemlik, Erdek, İzmir, Kuşadası, Bodrum and Marmaris can be considered ideal places for campers and caravanners. Other camping sites can usually be found in the vicinity of filling stations.

Before camping on private land, one should get the owner's permission.

There are also summer holiday centres which welcome tourists all through the summer months with comfortable holiday-camp accommodation with either full or half board for a reasonable charge.

Camping vocabulary

axe	balta	camp	kamp
air mattress	havayla şişirilmiş şilte	camp-bed	kamp yatağı
		camping equipment	kamp malzemesi
blanket	battaniye		
bottle opener	şişe açacağı	camping site	kamp yeri
bucket	kova	candle	mum

KEY TO PRONUNCIATION

c (jar), ç (church), g (gale), ğ (lengthen the preceding vowel), h (hill), ı (Cyril), j (Fr. *jeune*), ö (Fr. *peu* or Ger. *Köln*), s (sister), ş (shoe), ü (Fr. *dune* or Ger. *Glück*)

Camping, caravanning and cycling

compass	pusla	oil stove	gaz ocağı
cooking utensils	mutfak aletleri	paraffin	parafin
		pen knife	çakı
corkscrew	tribüşon, açacak	pick	kazma
cup	fincan	picnic	piknik, kır yemeği
drinking water	içecek su, içme suyu	pillow	yastık
		plate	tabak
fork	çatal	ruck sack	arka torbası
frying pan	tava	saucepan	saplı tencere
glass	bardak	shovel	kürek
ground sheet	çadır altına serilen örtü	shower	duş
		sleeping bag	uyku torbası, zipli kamp yorganı
hitch-hike, to	taşıtla parasız yolculuk etmek	spirit stove	ispirto ocağı
hut	kulübe	spoon	kaşık
kettle	tencere, çaydanlık	tent	çadır
knife	bıçak	tent-peg	çadır kazığı
log	kütük	tent-pole	çadır direği
map	harita	tent-rope	çadır ipi
matches	kibrit	thermos	termos şişesi
methylated spirits	metil gazı	tin opener	konserve kutusu açacağı
mosquito net	cibinnik	torch	elfeneri, meşale
moss	yosun	waterproof	su geçirmez
mountain refuge	dağ sığınağı		

Caravanning vocabulary

awning	tente, sayvan	coupling	bağlama, birleştirme
awning pole	tente direği		
bed	yatak	curtain	perde
blind	perde, jaluzi	curtain rail	perde rayı
bolt	sürgü, mandal	door fastener	kapı menteşesi
brace	çevirme kolu	door handle	kapı tokmağı
brakes	frenler	electric bulb	ampul

KEY TO PRONUNCIATION

c (jar), ç (church), g (gale), ğ (lengthen the preceding vowel), h (hill), ı (Cyril), j (Fr. *jeune*), ö (Fr. *peu* or Ger. *Köln*), s (sister), ş (shoe), ü (Fr. *dune* or Ger. Glück)

Camping, caravanning and cycling

electric plug	elektrik fişi	linoleum	linolyum
electric plug socket	priz	locker	dolap
		mat	hasır, paspas
electric wire	elektrik teli	mudguard	çamurluk
fibre-glass	fayberglas-kırılmaz cam	number plate lamp	plaka lambası
fire-extinguisher	yangın söndürme cihazı	nut	vida, somun
		paint	boya
folding bed	katlanan yatak	plastic	plastik
folding door	katlanan kapı	plastic foam	plastik köpüğü
gas	havagazı, gaz	pressure cooker	düdüklü tencere
gas cooker	havagazı ocağı, gazocağı		
		pump	pompa
gas fire	havagazı ateşi	reading lamp	okuma lambası
gas globe	havagazı kabı	rear lamp	arka lambası
gas lamp	gaz lambası	roof	dam, çatı
gas oven	havagazı fırını	roof lamp	çatı lambası
gas ring	havagazı çemberi	rubbish bin	çöp tenekesi
grill	ızgara	screw	vida
gutter	hendek, su yolu, oluk	seat	oturacak yer
		shade lamp	gece lambası
gutter drain-pipe	kanalizasyon	shelf	raf
		sink	bulaşık yıkama yeri, mecra
guy line	direği tesbit teli		
handle	kulp	sink drain-pipe	bulaşık oluğu
hinge	menteşe, reze		
hitch	bağ, ilişme	sink plug	bulaşık tıkaçı
insulation	tecrit, izolasyon	springs	yaylar
jockey wheel	karavanın öndeki küçük tekcrlcği	switch	elektrik düğmesi, devre anahtarı
key	anahtar	table leg	masa ayağı
kitchen	mutfak	table-leg stay	masa ayağı rabtedicisi
larder	kiler, erzak		
light	ışık	toilet room	tuvalet, yüz numara
light adjuster	ışık ayarlayıcısı		

KEY TO PRONUNCIATION

c (jar), ç (church), g (gale), ğ (lengthen the preceding vowel), h (hill), ı (Cyril), j (Fr. *jeune*), ö (Fr. *peu* or Ger. *Köln*), s (sister), ş (shoe), ü (Fr. *dune* or Ger. Glück)

Camping, caravanning and cycling

tow, to	çekmek
tow bar	çekme kolu
towing bracket	çekme birleştiricisi, sürgüsü
trailer plate	treyler plakası
ventilator	vantilatör
wardrobe	gardrop, elbise dolabı
washer	yıkayıcı, yekama cihazı, rondela
washer rubber	lastikten delikli pul
water-carrier	saka, su taşıyıcı
water pump	tulumba
wheel brace	tekerlek çevirme kolu
window latch	pencere mandalı
window-sill	pencere eşiği, pervazı
window valence	pencere kornişi

Cycling vocabulary

bottom bracket	alt dirsek, alt kol
brake cable	fren kablosu, fren teli
brake rod	fren çubuğu, fren kolu
chain	zincir
chain wheel	zincir çemberi
cycle, to	bisiklete binmek
dynamo lighting	elektrik dinamosu
frame	çatı, çerçeve
front brake	ön fren
front fork	ön çatal
grip	tutak yeri, pençe
handlebar	gidon, bisiklet idare kolu
hub	tekerlek göbeği, poyrası
lamp	lamba
luggage carrier	yük taşıma yeri
leather saddle-bag	meşin yük çantası
mudguard	çamurluk
pedal	pedal
rim	tekerlek çemberi
rear brake	arka fren
rear reflector	arka reflektör
saddle	sela, oturma yeri
spoke	tekerlek teli
tool kit	alet çantası
tyre (cover and inner)	lastik (dış ve iç)
valve	supap
wheel	tekerlek

Phrases

We are cycling.	Biz bisikletle seyahat ediyoruz.
We are travelling on foot.	Yürüyerek seyahat ediyoruz.

KEY TO PRONUNCIATION

c (jar), ç (church), g (gale), ğ (lengthen the preceding vowel), h (hill), ı (Cyril), j (Fr. *jeune*), ö (Fr. *peu* or Ger. *Köln*), s (sister), ş (shoe), ü (Fr. *dune* or Ger. Glück)

Camping, caravanning and cycling

We have no luggage.	Eşyamız yok.
We use our saddle-bags.	Meşin çantamızı kullanıyoruz.
Where does this road lead?	Bu yol nereye gider?
Are we on the right road to ...?	... 'e giden doğru yolda mıyız?
How long does it take to ...?	... 'e gitmek ne kadar sürer?
What is the name of this place?	Bu yerin adı nedir?
Can you show me on the map?	Haritada gösterebilir misiniz?
I should like to wash.	Temizlenmek istiyorum.
Is this drinking water?	Bu su içilebilir mi?
We're looking for somewhere to camp.	Kamp kuracak bir yer arıyoruz.
We're looking for the camping site.	Kamp yerini arıyoruz.
Can you direct us to the camping (caravan) site?	Bize kamp yerini (karavan yerini) gösterebilir misiniz?
Will you permit me to camp (caravan) here?	Burada kamp kurmama müsaade eder misiniz?
Where is the caravan site?	Karavanların kamp yeri nerede?
Where are we now on the map?	Haritada şimdi neredeyiz?
Where is the owner's office?	Kamp idarecisinin Bürosu nerede?
What is the charge per night?	Gecesi kaça ...?
— car.	— otomobilin.
— tent.	— çadırın.
— caravan.	— karavanın.
— person.	— adam başına.
Is the ground firm in wet weather?	Yağmurlu havalarda toprak sıkı durur mu?
Can I place my caravan here?	Karavanımı buraya koyabilir miyim?
Where are the toilets?	Tuvaletler nerede?
Are baths available?	Banyo yapılabilir mi?
Are there points for electric shavers?	Elektrikli traş makineleri için priz var mı?
Where can I dispose of waste water?	Kirli suyumu nereye dökebilirim?

KEY TO PRONUNCIATION

c (jar), ç (church), g (gale), ğ (lengthen the preceding vowel), h (hill), ı (Cyril), j (Fr. *jeune*), ö (Fr. *peu* or Ger. *Köln*), s (sister), ş (shoe), ü (Fr. *dune* or Ger. Glück)

Camping, caravanning and cycling

Where do I dispose of rubbish?	Çöpü nereye dökebilirim?
Is there a laundry for	Bir çamaşırlık var mı
— washing?	— yıkama için?
— drying?	— kurutma için?
— ironing clothes?	— ütülemek için elbiseleri?
Can batteries be charged on the site?	Kamp yerinde aküler şarj edilebilir mi?
Here is my camping carnet.	İşte kamp karnem.
Is there a camp shop?	Kampın dükkânı var mı?
At what time does the camp shop open (close)?	Kamp dükkânı saat kaçta açılır? (kapanır)?
Do tradesmen call at the site with bread or milk?	Ekmek veya süt satan esnaf kamp yerine gelir mi?
Where are the nearest shops to the site?	Kamp yerine en yakın pazar nerede?
Where is the nearest petrol station, please?	En yakın benzinci nerede, lütfen?
Can you tell me where I can buy camping equipment?	Nereden kamp malzemesi satın alabileceğimi söyler misiniz?
I have a puncture in the caravan tyre.	Karavanımın lastiği patladı.
Can you mend it?	Tamir edebilir misiniz?
The ... is broken. Can you mend it?	... kırıldı (bozuldu). Tamir edebilir misiniz?
Where can I buy newspapers?	Nereden gazete satın alabilirim?
Are there mosquitoes?	Sivrisinek var mı?
Can you recommend a cheap restaurant?	Ucuz bir lokanta sağlık verebilir misiniz?
We are leaving early tomorrow. Please let me have my bill.	Yarın sabah erkenden gidiyoruz. Lütfen hesabımı veriniz.
— my camping carnet.	— kamp karnemi veriniz.
— my passport now.	— lütfen pasaportumu şimdi veriniz.
Can you change dollars?	Dolar bozabilir misiniz?
— pounds.	— sterlin.

KEY TO PRONUNCIATION

c (jar), ç (church), g (gale), ğ (lengthen the preceding vowel), h (hill), ı (Cyril), j (Fr. *jeune*), ö (Fr. *peu* or Ger. *Köln*), s (sister), ş (shoe), ü (Fr. *dune* or Ger. *Glück*)

Camping, caravanning and cycling

Can one cash a traveller's cheque?	Travelers çek bozdurabilir miyim?
Do you charge for hot water?	Sıcak su için ayrıca para alıyor musunuz?
Where can I buy ice?	Nereden buz satın alabilirim?
Is there a deep freeze where I can have my camping ice frozen?	Kamping buzumu dondurabilecek bir buz dolabı var mı?
Can one buy fresh eggs in the camp store?	Kamp dükkânında taze yumurta bulunur mu?
Can one buy vegetables in the shop?	Kamp dükkânında sebze bulunur mu?
Is there butter in the camp shop?	Kamp dükkânında tereyağ var mı?
Can one buy souvenirs in the shop?	Kamp dükkânında hatıra eşyası bulunur mu?

KEY TO PRONUNCIATION

c (jar), ç (church), g (gale), ğ (lengthen the preceding vowel), h (hill), ı (Cyril), j (Fr. *jeune*), ö (Fr. *peu* or Ger. *Köln*), s (sister), ş (shoe), ü (Fr. *dune* or Ger. Glück)

11 Hotels

General

In Turkey hotels are graded according to the standards they maintain. The charges are fixed by law. Hotel rates are on the whole quite reasonable.

The hotels are classified as follows: *De luxe* hotels, first-class hotels, second-class hotels, third-class hotels and fourth-class hotels.

Besides these establishments there are numerous motels, guest houses and holiday villages.

The Ministry of Culture and Tourism issues an hotel guide every year announcing facilities available and charges for each and every type of accommodation. These guides may be obtained from Turkish Tourism and Information Offices free of charge.

Some private houses also provide bed and breakfast facilities in certain towns, and their charges are less than that of an hotel.

There are also youth-hostels where one can stay during the summer months at a very reasonable price.

It is always advisable to call at the Turkish Tourism Information Office in your country or ask your travel agent, who will be but too pleased to recommend accommodation to suit your pleasure.

Vocabulary on hotels, laundry and cleaning

air-conditioning	ısıyı ayarlama erkondişin	bath	banyo
		bathtub	banyo teknesi
armchair	koltuk	bathroom	banyo odası,
ashtray	küllük		hamam

KEY TO PRONUNCIATION

c (jar), ç (church), g (gale), ğ (lengthen the preceding vowel), h (hill), ı (Cyril), j (Fr. *jeune*), ö (Fr. *peu* or Ger. *Köln*), s (sister), ş (shoe), ü (Fr. *dune* or Ger. Glück)

Hotels

bed	yatak	chambermaid	hizmetçi kız, famdöşambr
bedroom	yatak odası		
single	tek yataklı	clothes	elbise, esvap
double	çift yataklı	coat hanger	elbise asacağı, askı
with twin beds	iki tek yataklı	collar	yaka
with double beds	iki kişilik yataklı	complaint	şikâyet
		cook	aşçı
bedspread	yatak örtüsü	cupboard	dolap
bedstead	karyola	curtain	perde
bed and breakfast	yatak ve kahvaltı	dining room	yemek odası, yemek salonu
bed and board	yatak ve yemek	enquiries	danışma, müracaat
bell	zil, çan, çıgırak	floor	kat, zemin
bellboy	belboy	girdle	korsa, kuşak
bellpull	çan ipi	hall	salon, hol, fuaye
belt	kuşak, kemer	head-waiter	başgarson, metrdotel
bill	fatura, hesap varakası	hook	çengel, kanca
blanket	battaniye	hotel	otel
blind	pancur, ıstor perde	hotel-keeper	otelci
		hot-water bottle	sıcaksu torbası
boarding house	pansiyon	iron, to	ütülemek
bolster	uzun yastık	iron	ütü
brassière	sutyen	jacket	caket
breakfast	kahvaltı	jumper	kazak, yünbluz, süveter
brush, to	fırçalamak		
brush	fırça	key	anahtar
bulb	ampul	lavatory	hela, aptesane, yüznumara
button	düğme		
central heating	kalorifer	lift	asansör
		lounge	dinlenme odası
chair	iskemle	management	idare, yönetim

KEY TO PRONUNCIATION

c (jar), ç (church), g (gale), ğ (lengthen the preceding vowel), h (hill), ı (Cyril), j (Fr. *jeune*), ö (Fr. *peu* or Ger. *Köln*), s (sister), ş (shoe), ü (Fr. *dune* or Ger. *Glück*)

manager	müdür	shutter	pancur
mend, to	tamir etme, yamalama	sitting room	oturma odası
		slip	kombinezon
mattress	şilte	socks	erkek çorabı
mirror	ayna	staircase	merdiven
nightdress	gecelik	stockings	kadın çorabı
office	ofis, büro	suit	erkek esvabı, tayyör
page-boy	otel garsonu, uşak		
pan (bedpan)	lâzımlık	suspender	pantalon askısı, jartiyer
petticoat	iç eteklik		
pillow	yastık	switch	elektrik düğmesi
plug	elektrik fişi	table	masa
porter	kapıcı	tablecloth	masa örtüsü
proprietor	otel sahibi, malsahibi	tap (hot, cold)	musluk (sıcaksu, soğuksu)
pullover	kolsuz kazak, kolsuz süveter	tourist hotel	turist oteli, turistik otel
pyjamas	pijama	towel	havlu
radiator	radyatör	trousers	pantalon
reading-lamp	başucu lambası	valet	vale
reception	resepsiyon	wardrobe	gardrop, dolap
scarf	eşarp	wash-basin	küvet
service	servis, hizmet	waste-paper basket	kâğıt sepeti
sheet	çarşaf		
shelf	raf	window	pencere
shirt	gömlek	zip-fastener	fermuar, zip
shower	duş		

Phrases

Please show me a good hotel.	Lütfen bana iyi bir otel gösteriniz.
Take me to a boarding-house.	Beni bir pansiyona götürünüz.
Is there a garage?	Garajı var mı?
I wrote to you a month ago. Is my room ready?	Size bir ay önce yazmıştım. Odam hazır mı?

KEY TO PRONUNCIATION

c (jar), ç (church), g (gale), ğ (lengthen the preceding vowel), h (hill), ı (Cyril), j (Fr. *jeune*), ö (Fr. *peu* or Ger. *Köln*), s (sister), ş (shoe), ü (Fr. *dune* or Ger. *Glück*)

Hotels

You promised to reserve a room with a bath for me.	Bana banyolu bir oda rezerve etmeğe söz vermiştiniz.
I want a room	Bir oda istiyorum
— with a single bed.	— tek yataklı.
— with two beds.	— çift yataklı.
— with a bathroom.	— banyolu.
— with shower.	— duşlu.
— without meals.	— yemeksiz.
— with breakfast only.	— sadece kahvaltılı.
— for one night only.	— sade bir gece için.
— facing south.	— güneye bakan.
— overlooking the sea.	— denize bakan.
— overlooking the garden.	— bahçeye bakan.
— for two weeks.	— iki hafta için.
Is there hot and cold running water in the room?	Odada sıcak ve soğuk akar su var mı?
Can I see the room?	Odayı görebilir miyim?
This room does not suit me.	Bu odayı beğenmedim.
This room suits me.	Bu odayı beğendim.
I shall stay for three nights.	Üç gece kalacağım.
Have you nothing better?	Daha iyi bir odanız yok mu?
What is the price of the room for the night?	Odanın bir gece için fiatı nedir?
Have you anything cheaper?	Daha ucuz bir odanız var mı?
How much do you charge per day including meals?	Yemekler dahil odanın günlük fiatı nedir?
How long do you intend to stay?	Ne kadar kalmağı düşünüyorsunuz?
How much reduction do I get if I stay more than a week?	Bir haftadan fazla kalırsam ne kadar tenzilat yaparsınız?
If I am pleased with it, I may stay for a fortnight.	Beğenirsem, iki hafta kalırım.
Here is the key of your room.	İşte odanızın anahtarı.
Is there a lift?	Asansör var mı?
I cannot sleep in this room, there is too much noise.	Bu odada uyuyamıyorum, çok gürültü var.

KEY TO PRONUNCIATION

c (jar), ç (church), g (gale), ğ (lengthen the preceding vowel), h (hill), ı (Cyril), j (Fr. *jeune*), ö (Fr. *peu* or Ger. *Köln*), s (sister), ş (shoe), ü (Fr. *dune* or Ger. *Glück*)

Can you give me a room on another floor?	Başka katta bir oda verebilir misiniz?
Please, send up my luggage at once.	Lütfen bavullarımı derhal odama gönderiniz.
My luggage is at the station, here is the ticket.	Bavullarım istasyonda, işte bileti.
Please call	Lütfen çağırınız
— the valet.	— valeyi.
— the chambermaid.	— famdöşambrı.
— the bell-boy.	— belboyu.
— the head-waiter.	— baş garsonu.
— the porter.	— kapıcıyı.
Where is the bathroom?	Banyo nerede?
I should like a hot bath.	Sıcak suyla banyo yapmak istiyorum.
There are no towels.	Havlu yok.
Please close the shutters.	Lütfen pancurları kapayınız.
Leave the window open.	Pencere açık kalsın.
May I have another pillow?	Bir yastık daha reca edebilir miyim?
I should like an extra blanket.	Bir battaniye daha istiyorum.
Please, wake me at eight a.m.	Lütfen beni saat sekizde kaldırınız.
Please bring me a bottle of mineral water.	Lütfen bir şişe maden suyu getiriniz.
I should like some iced water.	Buzlu su reca ediyorum.
Can you bring me a hot-water bottle, please.	Lütfen bir sıcak su torbası getirebilir misiniz?
Is there a plug for my electric shaver?	Traş makinem için bir priz var mı?
What is the voltage?	Elektrik voltajı ne kadar?
The light is very poor in the bathroom.	Banyoda ışık çok sönük.
Can you replace this bulb?	Bu ampulu değiştirebilir misiniz?
The radiator seems to be out of order.	Radyatör işlemiyor galiba.

KEY TO PRONUNCIATION

c (jar), ç (church), g (gale), ğ (lengthen the preceding vowel), h (hill), ı (Cyril), j (Fr. *jeune*), ö (Fr. *peu* or Ger. *Köln*), s (sister), ş (shoe), ü (Fr. *dune* or Ger. Glück)

Hotels

The radiator is too hot, will you please turn it off.	Radyatör son derece kızmış, lütfen kapatınız.
Are you the chamber-maid?	Fam döşambr siz misiniz?
Please sew on this button.	Lütfen bu düğmeyi dikiniz.
— brush this suit.	— bu elbiseyi fırçalayınız.
— iron this shirt.	— bu gömleği ütüleyiniz.
I shall be going out soon.	Birazdan dışarı çıkacağım.
I shall be back at five.	Beşte dönmüş olacağım.
If anyone asks for me, please tell them to wait.	Beni soran olursa, lütfen beklemelerini söyleyiniz.
I am expecting a lady.	Bir Bayan bekliyorum.
Has anyone called to see me?	Beni kimse aradı mı?
Has there been a telephone call for me?	Beni telefondan aradılar mı?
Is there a letter for me?	Bana mektup var mı?
Have you asked their telephone number?	Telefonlarının numarasını sordunuz mu?
Was there a message?	Bir haber bıraktılar mı?
Will you get this number for me, please?	Lütfen, bu numarayı bana bağlıyabilir misiniz?
Where should I leave my key?	Anahtarımı nereye bırakayım?
What time does the hotel close?	Otel kaçta kapanıyor?
Are you open all night?	Bütün gece açık mısınız?
Can I have breakfast in my room?	Kahvaltıyı odamda yapabilir miyim?
Can you put another bed in the room for the child?	Çocuk için odaya bir yatak daha koyabilir misiniz?
The room has not been cleaned.	Oda temizlenmemiş.
My shoes need polishing.	Ayakkabılarımın boyaya ihtiyacı var.
Please have these shoes cleaned.	Ayakkabılarımı temizlettiriniz.
I am not happy with the room service.	Oda servisinden memnun değilim.
I want to lodge a complaint with the manager.	Müdüre şikâyet etmek istiyorum.

KEY TO PRONUNCIATION

c (jar), ç (church), g (gale), ğ (lengthen the preceding vowel), h (hill), ı (Cyril), j (Fr. *jeune*), ö (Fr. *peu* or Ger. *Köln*), s (sister), ş (shoe), ü (Fr. *dune* or Ger. Glück)

Hotels

Have you seen my . . . ?	. . . mi gördünüz mü?
Please give me another towel.	Lütfen bir başka havlu veriniz.
Will you please bring me some soap?	Lütfen sabun getiriniz.
Where did you put my suitcase?	Bavulumu nereye koydunuz?
I have to leave early tomorrow.	Yarın erkenden gideceğim.
Please prepare my bill.	Lütfen hesabımı hazırlayınız.
I am taking the first plane.	İlk uçağa yetişeceğim.
I shall need a taxi for the air terminal.	Hava terminaline kadar bir taksi lazım.
Will you accept a traveller's cheque?	Travelers çek kabul eder misiniz?
Will you accept dollars?	Dolar kabul eder misiniz?
— pounds sterling?	Sterlin kabul eder misiniz?
Please correct my bill.	Lütfen hesabımı düzeltiniz.
Are the tips included?	Bahşış dahil mi?
The bill does not seem to agree with our arrangement.	Hesap anlaşmamıza uygun olarak hazırlanmamış.
Please forward my mail to this address.	Lütfen mektuplarımı şu adrese gönderiniz.
Please have the luggage brought down.	Lütfen bavullarımı aşağıya getirtiniz.
Is the taxi here?	Taksi geldi mi?
I have left my umbrella in the room.	Şemsiyemi odada bırakmışım.
Here is the key. Will you please fetch my hat?	Işte anahtar, lütfen şapkamı getirebilir misin?
I have left the key in the door.	Anahtarı kapının üstünde bıraktım.
Have you put all my luggage in the car?	Bütün eşyalarımı otomobile yerleştirdin mi?
Thank you! Keep it.	Teşekkür ederim. Sende kalsın!
Good-bye, sir. Come again!	Güle güle efendim. Yine buyrunuz!

KEY TO PRONUNCIATION

c (jar), ç (church), g (gale), ğ (lengthen the preceding vowel), h (hill), ı (Cyril), j (Fr. *jeune*), ö (Fr. *peu* or Ger. *Köln*), s (sister), ş (shoe), ü (Fr. *dune* or Ger. Glück)

Hotels

Overnight stay

I have missed my bus.	Otobüsümü kaçırdım.
— my plane.	— uçağımı kaçırdım.
— my train.	— trenimi kaçırdım.
Where can I spend the night?	Geceyi nerede geçirebilirim?
Is there a small hotel where I can stay?	Kalabileceğim küçük bir otel var mı?
I don't mind a youth hostel.	Bir öğrenci yurdu da olur.
Do you know a house nearby where we can stay?	Civarda kalabileceğimiz bir ev biliyor musunuz?
I'd like to stay here overnight.	Burada gecelemek istiyorum.
Can you put me up for the night?	Gece burada kalabilir miyim?
Have you got a room where I can stay?	Kalabileceğim bir oda var mı?
Any room will do.	Oda nasıl olursa olsun, farketmez.
Would you like me to pay in advance?	Parayı peşin ödememi ister misiniz?
I have left my luggage at the station.	Eşyamı istasyonda emanete bıraktım.
There is only my briefcase.	Sadece çantam var.
Can you recommend a modest restaurant?	Ortahalli bir lokanta tavsiye edebilir misiniz?
I shall leave early in the morning.	Sabah erkenden gideceğim.
Can you provide me with a picnic lunch, please?	Bana bir kır yemeği paketi hazırlıyabilir misiniz, lütfen?
Please call me at six in the morning.	Lütfen beni sabah saat altıda uyandırınız.
No, I shall not need a taxi.	Hayır, taksiye lüzum yok.

Post

Is there a post office in the hotel?	Otelde postane var mı?
Where is the post office?	Postane nerede?
Have you stamps?	Pul var mı?
How much does it cost to send a letter to England?	İngiltereye mektup kaç paraya gidiyor?

KEY TO PRONUNCIATION
c (jar), ç (church), g (gale), ğ (lengthen the preceding vowel), h (hill), ı (Cyril), j (Fr. *jeune*), ö (Fr. *peu* or Ger. *Köln*), s (sister), ş (shoe), ü (Fr. *dune* or Ger. *Glück*)

How much is it for U.S.A.?	Amerikaya ne kadar?
How much does it cost to send a postcard?	Kartpostal kaça gidiyor?
Where is the letter-box?	Posta kutusu nerede?
I want to send a telegram.	Bir tel göndermek istiyorum.
Do you accept cables here?	Burada tel kabul ediyor musunuz?
I want to telephone.	Telefon etmek istiyorum.
Which phone should I use?	Hangi telefonu kullanayım?
This telephone is out of order.	Bu telefon bozuk.
Am I wanted on the phone?	Beni telefondan mı arıyorlar?

Laundry and cleaning

I have some things to be washed.	Yıkanacak bazı şeylerim var.
Can I have them back this evening?	Akşama geri alabilir miyim?
When will they be ready?	Ne zaman hazır olur?
I must have them by Friday.	Cumaya almam lazım.
Please have these clothes dry-cleaned.	Lütfen bu elbiseleri kuru temizlemeye veriniz.
Please bring me a laundry list.	Lütfen bir çamaşır listesi getiriniz.
How soon can you have my shirts washed?	Gömleklerimi ne kadar zamanda yıkatabilirsiniz?

KEY TO PRONUNCIATION

c (jar), ç (church), g (gale), ğ (lengthen the preceding vowel), h (hill), ı (Cyril), j (Fr. *jeune*), ö (Fr. *peu* or Ger. *Köln*), s (sister), ş (shoe), ü (Fr. *dune* or Ger. Glück)

12 Meals and restaurants

Food in general

Turkish cuisine is one of the world's three primary cuisines. It is as famous as the Chinese and French cuisines. Turkey is renowned for the variety of its cooking. Its main characteristic is that unlike Oriental cuisine, it makes very modest use of spices. Turkish cooking does not tend to be heavy and rich as is often imagined.

In luxury-class restaurants in Istanbul, Ankara and İzmir, fresh fish from the sea is served to suit every palate – Kılıç balığı (sword-fish), çipura, levrek (bass), barbunya (red mullet) are some of the delicious fish dishes. Fresh fruit in season comes from all parts of Turkey – strawberries from Ereğli; honeylip figs and seedless grapes from İzmir; big, luscious peaches from Bursa; green pears from Ankara; oranges, tangerines, grapefruits and bananas from the Turquoise Coast of Turkey; melons and water-melons from the interior.

Kebabs (şiş, döner, kâğıt) small pieces of tender lamb grilled over a charcoal fire – sliced lamb similarly prepared – are great favourites with tourists.

Most soup and desserts are similar to those in Western Europe although some desserts such as baklava – crisp pastry with a layer of nuts and served in heavy syrup, helva – a confection of chopped nuts, sesame and honey, and güllâç – a sweet of wafers, ground almonds cooked in milk, are solely Turkish.

Turkish national dishes

International cuisine is featured by most large hotels and restaurants in important towns, but it is worth-while for the tourist to taste some of the Turkish specialities. Here is a short list of some of the national dishes (in alphabetical order):

KEY TO PRONUNCIATION
c (jar), ç (church), g (gale), ğ (lengthen the preceding vowel), h (hill), ı (Cyril), j (Fr. *jeune*), ö (Fr. *peu* or Ger. *Köln*), s (sister), ş (shoe), ü (Fr. *dune* or Ger. Glück)

Börek	Small rolls or triangles of pastry stuffed with cheese or minced meat and onions.
Çerkes tavuğu	Boiled and stripped chicken served with special thick walnut sauce flavoured with paprika.
Döner kebab	Mutton and lamb broiled on a roasting vertical spit, sliced thinly and served with pilav.
Dolma	Vine leaves or vegetables such as aubergine, peppers and tomatoes stuffed with rice, nuts and currants cooked in olive oil.
Hünkâr beyendi	Roasted meat with mashed (*purée*) aubergines.
İmam bayıldı	Whole aubergines, stuffed with chopped tomatoes and onions, cooked in olive oil and served cold.
İşkembe çorbası	A soup prepared with chopped tripe and egg sauce, a favourite cure for hangovers.
Kılıç balığı	Swordfish dressed with bay leaves and tomatoes and peppers and grilled on skewers over a charcoal fire.
Midye dolması	Mussels stuffed with spiced rice and cooked in olive oil, served cold.
Şiş kebabı	Cubes of mutton broiled on skewers with peppers and tomatoes served usually with pilav and vegetables.

Drinks

Water

Bottled spring water in Turkey is perfectly safe to drink and its taste is delicious. Mineral waters are also very popular. Besides the modern soft drinks, such as Coca-Cola, Pepsi-Cola, lemonade, orangeade, 7-Up, there are some national drinks which are usually worth trying.

Ayran	Whipped yogurt served with ice.
Boza	Made of fermented wheat and served with cinnamon on it.
Şıra	Grape cordial.
Salep	Dried orchis root in hot milk sprinkled with cinnamon. A popular winter drink.
Şerbet	Sweetened and iced fruit juices of different kinds.

KEY TO PRONUNCIATION

c (jar), ç (church), g (gale), ğ (lengthen the preceding vowel), h (hill), ı (Cyril), j (Fr. *jeune*), ö (Fr. *peu* or Ger. *Köln*), s (sister), ş (shoe), ü (Fr. *dune* or Ger. *Glück*)

Meals and restaurants

Coffee

Turkish coffee is made of fine-ground coffee boiled with water and sugar in a special pot called cezve and served in small cups. It is advisable to specify the degree of sweetness required – Sade (without sugar), Orta şekerli (medium) and Şekerli (sweet). Turkish coffee is served throughout the country, when coffee is ordered. Large hotels and *de-luxe* restaurants serve European coffee.

Tea

Tea in teapot, with milk and sugar, may be had in big cafés and hotels in the main towns. In tea-shops, samovar tea is popular. This is served in small glass cups and drunk without milk.

Wine

Most Turkish wines are very palatable to western tastes. Once they used to adorn the tables of Roman Emperors. Some of the well-known makes are Kavaklıdere, Doluca, Trakya, and Buzbağ both red and white. Although they cannot compare with the best French and German wines, connoisseurs say they are superior to all other European wines.

Liqueurs

Turkish liqueurs made from various fruits are delicious and quite popular. There are over a dozen different makes, all about 40 per cent alcohol.

Rakı

Rakı is the national drink, distilled from grapes and flavoured with aniseed, taken as an aperitif. It turns milk white when water is added. It is strong (40–50 per cent proof alcohol) and should be drunk neat followed by a glass of cold water.

Beer

Turkish beer, locally brewed in Istanbul and Ankara, is a lager beer and is served cold.

Alcoholic drinks may be bought and consumed at all hours. Lunch is served between noon and 2 p.m. and dinner between 7.30 and 10.30 p.m. Establishments serving food are – Lokanta, Gazino, Kebapçı,

KEY TO PRONUNCIATION

c (jar), ç (church), g (gale), ğ (lengthen the preceding vowel), h (hill), ı (Cyril), j (Fr. *jeune*), ö (Fr. *peu* or Ger. *Köln*), s (sister), ş (shoe), ü (Fr. *dune* or Ger. Glück)

Birahane, Pastahane. There are also many snack-bars and night clubs where one can have something to eat. Prices at all these food-serving establishments are fixed by law, though they vary with the class of the place. Menus are often printed in French or English at the restaurants in major cities. In smaller towns when you cannot understand the menu, you are welcome to visit the kitchen and order what you prefer.

Vocabulary–General

At the table

ashtray	tabla, küllük	napkin	peçete
bar	bar	olive-oil	zeytin yağı
bill	hesap, fatura	pastry-shop	pastane
bottle	şişe	pepper	biber
café	kahve	plate	tabak
chair	iskemle	restaurant	lokanta
coffee-pot	cezve	salt	tuz
cork	mantar	saucer	salçalık
corkscrew	açacak, tribüşon	serviette, napkin	peçete
cup	fincan	spoon	kaşık
fork	çatal	table	masa
glass	bardak	table-cloth	masa örtüsü
hungry, to be	acıkmak	table-spoon	yemek kaşığı
knife	bıçak	tea-pot	çaydanlık
meal	yemek	thirsty, to be	susamak
menu	yemek listesi, mönü	tip	bahşış
		toothpick	kürdan
milk-jug	süt kabı	vinegar	sirke
mustard	hardal	water-jug	sürahi

Vocabulary–Drinks

ayran	ayran (whipped yogurt served cold)	boza	boza (made of fermented wheat sprinkled with cinnamon)
beer	bira		

KEY TO PRONUNCIATION

c (jar), ç (church), g (gale), ğ (lengthen the preceding vowel), h (hill), ı (Cyril), j (Fr. *jeune*), ö (Fr. *peu* or Ger. *Köln*), s (sister), ş (shoe), ü (Fr. *dune* or Ger. Glück)

Meals and restaurants

brandy	konyak	rakı	rakı (grape brandy flavoured with aniseed)
chocolate	çikolata		
Coca-cola	koka-kola		
cocoa	kakao	red wine	kırmızı şarap
coffee	kahve	salep	salep (dried orchis root in hot milk sprinkled with cinnamon)
cognac	konyak		
fruit juice	meyva suyu		
ice	buz		
ice-cream	dondurma	soda water	soda
iced water	buzlu su	Shira	şira (grape cordial)
lemonade	limonata	sherbet	şerbet (all kinds of soft fruit drinks)
liqueur	likör		
milk	süt	tea	çay
mineral water	maden suyu	water	su
		white wine	beyaz şarap
orangeade	portakal suyu	wine	şarap

Ways of cooking

baked in paper	kâğıtta pişmiş	medium	orta pişmiş
boiled	haşlama	on the spit	şişte
cold	söğüş	on the skewer	dönerde
fried	tavada kızartma	roast	fırında kızartma
grilled	ızkara	underdone	az pişmiş
		well done	iyi pişmiş

Terms on the menu

a bottle	bir şişe	main dishes	antreler
appetizers	mezeler	salads	salatalar
desserts	tatlılar	sauces	salçalar
drinks	meşrubat	sea food	deniz yemekleri (balıklar)
fruits	meyvalar		
half a bottle	yarım şişe	soups	çorbalar
hors d'oeuvres	mezeler (ordövr)	today's special	günün yemeği
		vegetables	sebzeler
in olive oil	zeytin yağlılar		

KEY TO PRONUNCIATION

c (jar), ç (church), g (gale), ğ (lengthen the preceding vowel), h (hill), ı (Cyril), j (Fr. *jeune*), ö (Fr. *peu* or Ger. *Köln*), s (sister), ş (shoe), ü (Fr. *dune* or Ger. *Glück*)

Vocabulary–Food

apple	elma	lobster	ıstakoz
apricot	kayısı	marmalade	marmalat
artichoke	enginar	macaroni	makarna
asparagus	kuşkonmaz	meat	et
aubergine	patlıcan	melon	kavun
banana	muz	mint	nane
beans	fasulye	mince	kıyma
biscuit	bisküvi	mushroom	mantar
bread	ekmek	mussels	midye
butter	tereyağ	mustard	hardal
cabbage	lahana	olive	zeytin
cake	pasta	olive-oil	zeytin yağ
carrot	havuç	omelette	omlet
cauliflower	karnıbahar	onion	soğan
cherries	kiraz	orange	portakal
cheese	peynir	parsley	maydanoz
crayfish	ıstakoz	pastry	pasta
cream	krema	peach	şeftali
cucumber	salatalık, hiyar	pear	armut
dolma	dolma—stuffed vine or cabbage leaves	peas	bezelye
		pepper	biber
		pie	börek, tatlı
egg	yumurta	plum	erik
fish	balık	potato	patates
fruit	meyva	puff pastry	börek
garlic	sarmısak	poultry	kümes hayvanı
grapes	üzüm	raspberries	ağaç çileği, ahududu
ham	jambon		
hare	tavşan eti	rice	pirinç, pilav
ice	buz	roll	ufak sarma ekmek
ice-cream	dondurma	salad	salata
jam	reçel	salami	salam
leek	pırasa	salmon	som balığı
lemon	limon	salt	tuz

KEY TO PRONUNCIATION

c (jar), ç (church), g (gale), ğ (lengthen the preceding vowel), h (hill), ı (Cyril), j (Fr. *jeune*), ö (Fr. *peu* or Ger. *Köln*), s (sister), ş (shoe), ü (Fr. *dune* or Ger. *Glück*)

Meals and restaurants

sauce	salça	tangerine	mandalina
sausage	sucuk	toast	kızarmış ekmek, tost
shrimp	karides		
snail	salyangoz	tomato	domates
sole	dil balığı	vanilla	vanilya
soup	çorba	vegetables	sebzeler
spinach	ıspanak	vinegar	sirke
strawberry	çilek	water-melon	karpuz
sugar	şeker	yoghurt	yoğurt

Kinds of cheese

cottage cheese	beyaz peynir	Cheddar	Kaşer
gruyère	gravyer	cheese in the skin	tulum peyniri

Kinds of bread

brown bread	ekmek	sandwich rolls	sandviç ekmeği
white bread	francala		
rye bread	çavdar ekmeği		

Kinds of sea-food

prawn cocktail	} karides kokteyl	stuffed mackerel	uskumru dolması
shrimp cocktail			
fried sprats	hamsi tava	grilled mackerel	uskumru ızgara
red mullet	barbunya	fried bass	levrek tavada
sword-fish	kılıç balığı	bass baked in paper	levrek kâğıtta
fried mussels	midye tava		
stuffed mussels	midye dolması	lobster	ıstakoz
loufer	lüfer		

Poultry and game

chicken	tavuk	duck	ördek
chick	piliç	duckling	palaz
deer	geyik	goose	kaz

KEY TO PRONUNCIATION

c (jar), ç (church), g (gale), ğ (lengthen the preceding vowel), h (hill), ı (Cyril), j (Fr. *jeune*), ö (Fr. *peu* or Ger. *Köln*), s (sister), ş (shoe), ü (Fr. *dune* or Ger. *Glück*)

gosling	palaz	rabbit	tavşan
partridge	keklik	turkey	hindi
pigeon	güvercin	wild duck	yaban ördeği
quail	bıldırcın	woodcock	çulluk

Kinds of meat

beef	sığır eti	slices carved off a thick wedge of meat roast on a vertical spit	döner kebap
cutlet	kotlet		
lamb	kuzu eti		
mutton	koyun eti		
pork	domuz eti	lady's thigh—fried meat balls	kadın budu köfte
veal	sığır		
steak	bonfile	roast lamb with spiced rice	kuzu dolması
chop	pirzola		
sausage	sucuk	small pieces of lamb placed on a spit and cooked over a glowing brazier	şiş kebap
Turkish sausage	sucuk		
roast beef	rozbif		
beefsteak	biftek		
minced meat	kıyma	a preserve of dried salt meat	pastırma
meat and rice balls	köfte		

Some sweets and desserts

aşure	a pudding made of boiled wheat, corn, sultanas, dry figs, hazel nuts and walnuts.
baklava	crisp pastry with a layer of nuts and served in heavy syrup.
dilber dudağı	lip-shaped pastry made from sponge-mixture and served with heavy syrup.
güllâç	a sweet of wafers, ground almonds cooked in milk.
helva	a confection of chopped nuts, sesame and honey.
kabak tatlısı	pumpkin cooked with sugar and served with pounded walnuts.
keşkül	a pudding made with milk, ground rice and sugar, browned in the oven and served with pistachio nuts.
lokum	Turkish Delight.

KEY TO PRONUNCIATION

c (jar), ç (church), g (gale), ğ (lengthen the preceding vowel), h (hill), ı (Cyril), j (Fr. *jeune*), ö (Fr. *peu* or Ger. *Köln*), s (sister), ş (shoe), ü (Fr. *dune* or Ger. *Glück*)

Meals and restaurants

mahallebi	same as keşkül, but prepared without rice and served with cinnamon.
sarığı burma	'Twisted Turban' – a kind of baklava in the shape of a turban.
sütlâç	a pudding with milk and rice.
vezir parmağı	'Vizier's Finger', a kind of sponge cake prepared in syrup in the shape of a finger.
zerde	kind of pudding prepared with rice and saffron. Usually served at wedding dinners.

Phrases

Please show me to a good restaurant.	Lütfen bana iyi bir lokanta gösteriniz. (sağlik veriniz.)
Please show us the best restaurant around here.	Lütfen bize buranın en iyi lokantasını gösteriniz.
What time is lunch?	Öğle yemeği saat kaçta?
— dinner?	Akşam yemeği saat kaçta?
Can you serve me quickly?	Bana çabuk servis yapabilir misiniz?
Give me the menu, please.	Lütfen, mönüyü veriniz.
Give me the wine list, please.	Lütfen şarap listesini veriniz.
What have you ready?	Hazır neyiniz var?
How much is the meal?	Yemek kaça?
Is there table d'hôte?	Tabldot var mı?
We are in a hurry. Can you serve at once?	Acelemiz var. Hemen servis yapabilir misin?
We want something light.	Hafif bir şey yemek istiyoruz.
We only want a snack.	Bir iki lokma bir şey istiyoruz.
We should like to have a table for four.	Dört kişilik bir masa istiyoruz.
I should like some soup.	Çorba istiyorum.
— some fish.	Balık istiyorum.
— some meat.	Et istiyorum.
Some salt and pepper, please.	Lütfen biraz tuz ve biber.
Some oil and vinegar, please.	Zeytinyağ ve sirke, lütfen.

KEY TO PRONUNCIATION

c (jar), ç (church), g (gale), ğ (lengthen the preceding vowel), h (hill), ı (Cyril), j (Fr. *jeune*), ö (Fr. *peu* or Ger. *Köln*), s (sister), ş (shoe), ü (Fr. *dune* or Ger. Glück)

No garlic, please.	Sarmısak olmasın, lütfen.
What have you got to drink?	İçecek neyiniz var?
Where can I wash my hands?	Ellerimi nerede yıkıyabilirim?
Where is the toilet?	Tuvalet nerede?
Waiter, bring us some bread, please.	Garson, lütfen bize ekmek getir.
What have you chosen?	Ne emredersiniz?
Please bring us some salad.	Lütfen bize salata getir.
What would you like to follow?	Sonra ne emredersiniz?
Please bring us some cold water.	Lütfen bize soğuk su getir.
I would like an ice-cream, please.	Dondurma istiyorum, lütfen.
I would like a glass of beer.	Bir bardak bira istiyorum.
— of fruit juice.	Bir bardak meyva suyu istiyorum.
— of lemonade.	Bir bardak limonata istiyorum.
— of ayran.	Bir bardak ayran istiyorum.
Is there milk for the child?	Çocuk için süt bulunur mu?
We would like some Turkish coffee.	Kahve istiyoruz.
Is the fish fresh?	Balık taze mi?
Please bring it without oil.	Zeytinyağ koymadan getiriniz.
— without sauce.	Salçasız olsun lütfen.
— without onions.	Sovansız olsun lütfen.
Could I have a little more, please.	Bir az daha reca edebilir miyim?
Please bring some more sugar.	Lütfen biraz daha şeker getiriniz.
— some more milk.	Lütfen biraz daha süt getiriniz.
— some more cream.	Lütfen biraz daha krema getiriniz.
— some more hot water.	Lütfen biraz daha sıcak su getiriniz.
— some more ice.	Lütfen biraz daha buz getiriniz.
The bill, please.	Hesabı, lütfen.
Are tips included?	Bahşış dahil mi?
There is a mistake in the bill.	Hesapta bir yanlışlık var.
We did not have bread.	Ekmek yemedik.
We did not have two bottles of beer.	İki şişe bira içmedik.

KEY TO PRONUNCIATION

c (jar), ç (church), g (gale), ğ (lengthen the preceding vowel), h (hill), ı (Cyril), j (Fr. *jeune*), ö (Fr. *peu* or Ger. *Köln*), s (sister), ş (shoe), ü (Fr. *dune* or Ger. Glück)

Meals and restaurants

What is that for?	Bu ne için?
I made a mistake.	Bir yanlışlık yapmışım.
I beg your pardon.	Özür dilerim.
My friend has left his ring in the toilet.	Arkadaşım yüzüğünü tuvalette bırakmış.
I have left my glasses in the toilet.	Gözlüklerimi tuvalette bırakmışım.
Where can I find a place to park the car?	Otomobili park edecek yer nerede bulabilirim?
Are you on a diet?	Perhiz mi yapıyorsunuz?
Yes, I am on a diet.	Evet, perhiz yapıyorum.
I would prefer something without olive oil in it.	Zeytinyağda pişmemiş bir yemeği tercih ederim.
I want something without too much fat in it.	Yağsız bir yemek istiyorum.
May I have cold chicken, please.	Tavuk sövüşü reca edebilir miyim?
May I have something very simple.	Çok sade bir şey verebilir misiniz?

KEY TO PRONUNCIATION

c (jar), ç (church), g (gale), ğ (lengthen the preceding vowel), h (hill), ı (Cyril), j (Fr. *jeune*), ö (Fr. *peu* or Ger. *Köln*), s (sister), ş (shoe), ü (Fr. *dune* or Ger. *Glück*)

13 Shopping

The principal cities in Turkey have excellent shopping facilities where all one's requirements may easily be obtained. Turkey produces beautifully coloured carpets and rugs with intricate designs; goat- and sheep-skin rugs; silver and copper ware; trinkets and filigree jewellery; wooden cigarette holders; wooden spoons; meerschaum pipes; onyx ware; suede coats; tiles and china ornaments; Turkish towels; glassware; hookahs (hubble-bubbles); and many other unusual souvenir crafts. In Istanbul the Covered Bazaar (Kapalı Çarşı) and the Spice Bazaar (Mısır Çarşısı) are delightful places for shopping. There one can see the examples of ancient crafts of Turkey – carpet-making, embroidery and ceramics.

Shopping hours on weekdays are from 9 in the morning until 7 in the evening with a lunch break from 1 p.m. to 2 p.m. Food shops are open until 9 p.m. in the evening. On Saturdays all shops are open until 9 p.m., though they observe an hour's lunch break from 1 to 2 p.m. when they are all closed.

A list of shopkeepers

antique dealer	antikacı	chemist	eczacı, eczane
baker	fırıncı	cleaner	temizleyici
baker's	ekmekçi	coppersmith	bakırcı
bank	banka	dairy	sütçü dükkânı, mahallebici
barber	berber		
bookshop	kitapçı, kitabevi	dressmaker	kadın terzisi
butcher	kasap	dry cleaner	kuru temizleyici
cake-shop	pastacı, pastane	electrician	elektrikçi
carpet-seller	halıcı	fishmonger	balıkçı

KEY TO PRONUNCIATION
c (jar), ç (church), g (gale), ğ (lengthen the preceding vowel), h (hill), ı (Cyril), j (Fr. *jeune*), ö (Fr. *peu* or Ger. *Köln*), s (sister), ş (shoe), ü (Fr. *dune* or Ger. Glück)

Shopping

florist	çiçekçi	milkman	sütçü
furrier	kürkçü	perfumery	parfümöri
glassware	zücaciyeci	photographic shop	fotografçı
goldsmith	kuyumcu		
greengrocer	manav	rug merchant	halıcı
grocer	bakkal	shoemaker	ayakkabıcı
haberdashery	tuhafiyeci, tuhafiye dükkânı	shoe repairer	ayakkabı tamircisi, pençeci
hairdresser	kuvaför, kadın berberi	shoeshop	ayakkabı dükkânı
ironmonger	hırdavatçı	souvenir craft	hatıra eşyası
jeweller	mücevherci, kuyumcu	stationer	kırtasiyeci
		tailor	terzi
leatherware	deri eşayası satan	tobacconist	tütüncü
		travel agent	turizm acentası
market	pazar	watchmaker	saatçi
meerschaum pipe-maker	lüleci	welder	kaynakçı
		wine merchant	şarapçı

Useful words

bag	çanta	cigarette	sigara
blade	traş bıçağı	coat	ceket
blouse	bluz	collar stud	yaka düğmesi
bracelet	bilezik	comb	tarak
braces	askı	cotton	pamuklu
brooch	broş	cotton wool	pamuk
brush	fırça	cuff links	kol düğmeleri
bulb	ampul, sovan	dark	koyu
button	düğme	dear	pahalı
cake of soap	bir kalıp sabun	dictionary	sözlük
card	kart	disinfectant	dezenfektan
cardboard	mukavva	doll	bebek
cheap	ucuz	dress	elbise
cigar	püro	earrings	küpeler

KEY TO PRONUNCIATION

c (jar), ç (church), g (gale), ğ (lengthen the preceding vowel), h (hill), ı (Cyril), j (Fr. *jeune*), ö (Fr. *peu* or Ger. *Köln*), s (sister), ş (shoe), ü (Fr. *dune* or Ger. Glück)

Shopping

elastic	elastiki	nail file	tırnak törpüsü
electric shaver	elektrikli traş makinesi	narrow	dar
		necklace	kolye, gerdanlık
embroidery	el işlemesi, nakış	neck-tie	boyunbağı, kıravat
envelope	zarf	needle	dikiş iğnesi
eau de cologne	kolonya	newspaper	gazete
girdle	korsa	pants	pantalon, iç donu
gloves	eldivenler		
guide-book	rehber kitap	panties	külot, kadın donu
handbag	para çantası		
handkerchief	mendil	paper	kağıt
hat	şapka	pen (ball point)	tükenmez kalem
heavy	ağır, kalın	pen (fountain)	dolma kalem
heel	topuk	pencil	kurşunkalem
ink	mürekkep	perfume	parfüm, koku
insecticide	haşaratı öldürecek ilaç	pair of socks	bir çift erkek çorabı
invisible mending	görünmez yama	pair of stockings	bir çift kadın çorabı
jacket	caket	powder box	pudra kutusu
label	etiket	purse	kese, bozukpara çantası
lace	dantela, şerit		
large	geniş, büyük	pin	iğne
light	açık, hafif	pipe	pipo
lighter	çakmak	plan	plan
lighter flint	çakmak taşı	raincoat	yağmurluk, pardesü
lighter fuel	çakmak benzini		
lipstick	dudak boyası, ruj	razor	ustura
		razor blades	traş bıçakları
long	uzun	ribbon	kurdele
magazine	mecmua, dergi	ring	yüzük
map	harita	sales	ucuz satış
matches	kibrit	sandals	sandal, çarık
material	kumaş, mal	scissors	makas

KEY TO PRONUNCIATION

c (jar), ç (church), g (gale), ğ (lengthen the preceding vowel), h (hill), ı (Cyril), j (Fr. *jeune*), ö (Fr. *peu* or Ger. *Köln*), s (sister), ş (shoe), ü (Fr. *dune* or Ger. Glück)

Shopping

self-service	selfservis	suitcase	bavul
shirt	gömlek	sun-hat	güneş şapkası
shaving brush	traş fırçası	sun-glasses	güneş gözlüğü
shaving lotion	traş losyonu	suspender	pantalon askısı,
shaving cream	traş kremi		askı, çorap
shoes	ayakkabılar		bağları
shoe-horn	çekecek	thick	kalın
shoe-laces	ayakkabı bağı	thimble	yüksük
shoe polish	ayakkabı boyası	thin	ince
shop	dükkân	thread	iplik
short	kısa	tight	sıkı
shorts	şort, kısa pantalon	tie	bağ
		toothbrush	diş fırçası
shawl	şal	tooth paste	diş macunu
silk	ipekli	towel	havlu
size	büyüklük, ölçü	tobacco	tütün
skirt	eteklik	torch	elfeneri
slippers	terlik	toy	oyuncak
small	küçük, ufak	trenchcoat	yağmurluk,
soap	sabun		empermeabl
sole	taban	trousers	pantalon
souvenir	hatıra	umbrella	şemsiye
spade	bahçıvan beli, maça	wallet	cüzdan
		watch	kolsaati
spectacles	gözlük	wide	geniş
stick	baston	wire	tel
strap	kayış	wool	yün, yünlü
string	sicim, ip	writing paper	yazı kâğıdı

Colours

azure	gök mavisi	bluish grey	gök elâ
beige	bej	brick	kiremit rengi
black	kara, siyah	brown	kahverengi
blue	mavi	crimson	al

KEY TO PRONUNCIATION

c (jar), ç (church), g (gale), ğ (lengthen the preceding vowel), h (hill), ı (Cyril), (Fr. *jeune*), ö (Fr. *peu* or Ger. *Köln*), s (sister), ş (shoe), ü (Fr. *dune* or Ge Glück)

dark	koyu	orange	turuncu
golden	altın rengi	pale green	tirşe
green	yeşil	peacock blue	cam göbeği
greenish grey	açık elâ	pink	pembe
grey	kurşuni, gri	purple	mor
indigo	çivit rengi	purplish brown	vişne çürüğü
ivory	fildişi rengi	plum	patlıcan rengi
lapis lazuli	lâcivert	red	kırmızı
light	açık	rosy	tozpembe
light brown	elâ	scarlet	kızıl
lilac coloured	eflâtun	silvery	gümüşü
lime green	fıstıki	white	beyaz, ak
mauve	eflatun	yellow	sarı

Phrases

At what time do the shops open?	Dükkânlar saat kaçta açılıyor?
At what time do the shops close?	Dükkânlar saat kaçta kapanıyor?
What can I do for you?	Ne emrediyorsunuz?
Are you being served?	Size bakıyorlar mı?
I want to buy ...	... satın almak istiyorum.
Do you sell ...?	... satıyor musunuz?
Where is the market?	Pazar nerede?
Have you anything cheaper?	Daha ucuz bir şey var mı?
Have you anything better?	Daha iyi bir şey var mı? or (Daha iyisi var mı?).
I want something like this?	Buna benzer bir şey istiyorum.
I would like something as a souvenir.	Hatıra olarak bir şey satın almak istiyorum.
How much is that?	Onun fiatı kaça?
I would like some post-cards.	Kartpostal almak istiyorum.
Have you anything bigger?	Bunun daha büyüğü var mı?
— smaller?	— küçüğü var mı?
— thicker?	— kalını var mı?
— thinner?	— incesi var mı?

KEY PTO RONUNCIATION

c (jar), ç (church), g (gale), ğ (lengthen the preceding vowel), h (hill), ı (Cyril), j (Fr. *jeune*), ö (Fr. *peu* or Ger. *Köln*), s (sister), ş (shoe), ü (Fr. *dune* or Ger. Glück)

Shopping

I prefer something in silk.	Ipekli bir şeyi tercih ederim.
— wool.	Yünlü bir şeyi tercih ederim.
— cotton.	Pamuklu bir şeyi tercih ederim.
— nylon.	Naylon bir şeyi tercih ederim.
How much does it cost a metre?	Bunun metresi kaça?
What width is it?	Bunun eni ne kadardır?
Would you please tell me its size?	Bunun boyunu söyliyebilir misiniz?
I want something longer.	Daha uzununu istiyorum.
Have you got a shorter one?	Daha kısası var mı?
Can I order it?	Ismarlıyabilir miyim?
Can you send it to this address?	Şu adrese gönderebilir misiniz?
Please make a parcel.	Lütfen paket yapınız.
I shall take them with me.	Paketi beraberimde götüreceğim.
Would you please tie the parcel?	Paketi sicimle bağlıyabilir misiniz?
Is this what you want?	İstediğiniz bu mu?
Yes, that is exactly what I want.	Evet, tam istediğim işte şu.
How much will that be altogether?	Hepsi ne ediyor?
Where shall I pay?	Parasını nereye ödiyeceğim?
May I leave the parcel here for a while?	Paketi bir müddet burada bırakabilir miyim?
I shall come back and collect it in half an hour.	Yarım saate kadar gelip alırım.
Do you have material to match this colour?	Bu renge uydurabilecek kumaşınız var mı?
This colour is too pale.	Bu renk çok soluk.
This colour is too loud.	Bu renk çok frapan (gözalıcı).
Does it lose colour in the wash?	Çamaşırda renk atar mı?
Could you keep it for me?	Bunu benim için ayırabilir misiniz?
Please show me something different.	Lütfen değişik bir şey gösteriniz.
I bought this yesterday. It doesn't fit me.	Bunu dün satın aldım. Bana uymuyor.

KEY TO PRONUNCIATION

c (jar), ç (church), g (gale), ğ (lengthen the preceding vowel), h (hill), ı (Cyril), j (Fr. *jeune*), ö (Fr. *peu* or Ger. *Köln*), s (sister), ş (shoe), ü (Fr. *dune* or Ger. *Glück*)

Would you please change it?	Lütfen değiştirebilir misiniz?
Can my money be refunded?	Param iade edilebilir mi?
Will you give me a reduction?	Bir tenzilât yapacak mısınız?
Do you sell leatherware?	Deri eşyası satıyor musunuz?
Where can I buy . . . ?	. . . nereden satın alabilirim?
Is it far from here?	Buradan uzak mı?
Would you please direct me to an antique dealer's shop?	Bana bir antikacı dükkânı gösterebilir misiniz?
Is there a hairdresser near here?	Bu civarda bir kadın berberi bulunur mu?
I want to buy some hand-embroidered scarves.	Elde işlenmiş şal satın almak istiyorum.
Are these hand-woven?	Bunlar elde mi örülmüş?
Where are the meerschaum-pipe makers?	Lüleci dükkânları ne tarafta?
Please write the name of the shop.	Lütfen dükkânın ismini yazınız.
Do you sell shirts here?	Gömlek satıyor musunuz?
Is this my size?	Bu benim boyum mu? (numaram mı?)
Do you sell leather jackets?	Deri ceket satıyor musunuz?
May I try it on?	Tecrübe edebilir miyim?
This is too big.	Bu çok büyük.
— long.	uzun.
— narrow.	— dar.
— short.	—kısa.
— small.	—küçük.
— wide.	— geniş.
Direct me to a greengrocer, please.	Lütfen bana bir manav dükkânı gösteriniz.
Do you sell oranges?	Portakal satıyor musunuz?
I want a kilogram of . . .	Bir kilo . . . istiyorum.
Are these Bursa peaches?	Bunlar Bursa şeftalisi mi?
How much are they per kilo?	Kilosu kaça?
That will do.	O kadar yeter.

KEY TO PRONUNCIATION

c (jar), ç (church), g (gale), ğ (lengthen the preceding vowel), h (hill), ı (Cyril), j (Fr. *jeune*), ö (Fr. *peu* or Ger. *Köln*), s (sister), ş (shoe), ü (Fr. *dune* or Ger. Glück)

Shopping 109

Would you let me choose my own?	Kendim seçebilir miyim?
Where can I buy some wine?	Nereden şarap satın alabilirim?
Do grocers sell wine in Turkey?	Türkiyede bakkallar şarap satar mı?
Give me a bottle of wine, please.	Lütfen, bana bir şişe şarap veriniz.
How much does this bottle cost?	Bu şişenin fiatı nedir?
No, not red. I'd rather have white.	Kırmızı değil. Beyazı tercih ediyorum.
Could I have a dozen eggs?	Bir düzine yumurta verebilir misin?
Are they fresh?	Taze mi?
Is this the cash desk?	Vezne burası mı?
Would you change this 1000 lira bill for me?	Şu bin lirayı bozabilir misiniz?
You have given me the wrong change.	Üstünü eksik verdiniz.
Thank you for helping me.	Yardımınıza teşekkür ederim.

Post Office and Telephone

Turkish Post Offices carry the letters PTT and use the colour gold as their emblem. Major Post Offices are open at 8 a.m. until 7 p.m.

Postal rates to Europe naturally vary in accordance with the weight of a letter. Up to 20 grammes it is 50 Tl. for a letter and 35 Tl. for a postcard. To USA a ten gramme letter costs 70 Tl., a 20 gramme letter costs 90 Tl. However, it is always advisable to check, either at the Post Office or at your hotel, the postal rate during your visit. For registered letters an additional charge of 200 Tl. is required.

For direct phone calls to England, one has to dial '9' and wait for a special continuous dialling tone, then dial '9', country code and the specific number uninterruptedly. Should the city number start with '0', one should ignore it. The country code from Turkey for England is 9 944 and USA is 9 91.

Telephone – For trunk calls, dial 03 and ask the operator for the

KEY TO PRONUNCIATION

c (jar), ç (church), g (gale), ğ (lengthen the preceding vowel), h (hill), ı (Cyril), j (Fr. *jeune*), ö (Fr. *peu* or Ger. *Köln*), s (sister), ş (shoe), ü (Fr. *dune* or Ger. *Glück*)

number you wish to call. Insert no money – you pay at the counter. There is a three-class preferential system for getting such calls through. If the call is person-to-person, an additional one-third is added to this price. Urgent calls are three times the normal rates and very urgent (Yıldırım) calls are five times the normal rates.

For Fire, one has to dial 00, for night-chemists 01, for telephone repairs 02, for long-distance calls 03, for telegrams 04, for TIM 05, and for long-distance tracer 06. (The 'long-distance tracer', 06, may be dialled after booking a long-distance call. By doing this one may find out how soon the connection will be made.)

Vocabulary

address	adres	postcard	kartpostal
airmail stamp	uçak pulu	postman	postacı
cable	telgraf, tel, kablo	postal order	posta havalesi
call	konuşma, mükâleme	post office	postane
		poste restante	post restan
call-box	(umumi telefon), telefon kulübesi	public telephone	genel telefon, umumi telefon
counter	tezgâh	register, to	taahhütlü göndermek
delivery	tevzi, teslim— dağıtım	registered	taahhütlü
directory (telephone)	telefon rehberi	reply paid	ödemeli
		sender	gönderen
letter	mektup	stamp	pul
letter-box	mektup kutusu	telegram	tel, telgraf
money order	para havalesi	telegraph office	telgrafhane
number	numara		
parcel	paket	telephone	telefon

Phrases

Where is the post office?	Postane nerede?
Is it near here?	Buraya yakın mı?
Where do I get postage stamps?	Nereden pul alabilirim?

KEY TO PRONUNCIATION

c (jar), ç (church), g (gale), ğ (lengthen the preceding vowel), h (hill), ı (Cyril), j (Fr. *jeune*), ö (Fr. *peu* or Ger. *Köln*), s (sister), ş (shoe), ü (Fr. *dune* or Ger. *Glück*)

Shopping

Where do they sell stamps?	Pul nerede satılıyor?
Give me a stamp for England.	İngiltere için bir pul veriniz.
Give me an airmail stamp for the U.S.A.	ABD için bir uçak pulu veriniz.
How much is it for England?	İngiltereye ne kadar?
How much is it for the U.S.A.?	Amerikaya ne kadar tutuyor?
I want this letter to go airmail.	Bu mektubu uçak postası göndermek istiyorum!
I want to register this letter.	Bu mektubu taahhütlü göndermek istiyorum.
How much is it for a postcard?	Kartpostal kaça gider?
I want to send this parcel.	Bu paketi göndermek istiyorum.
Would you give me a receipt for my registered letter?	Taahhütlü mektubum için bir makbuz verecek misiniz?
How much more should I pay for an express letter?	Ekspres mektup için ne kadar fazla ödemem lazım?
May I have a telegram form, please?	Lütfen bir telgraf kâğıdı verebilir misiniz?
What is the telegram rate to England?	İngiltereye telin kelimesi kaça?
Have you a letter poste-restante for me?	Bana postrestan bir mektup var mı?
Please forward my mail to ...	Lütfen mektuplarımı şu adrese postalayınız.
I wish to telephone locally.	Şehir içi telefon etmek istiyorum.
Please get me this number.	Lütfen şu numarayı bağlayınız.
It is the wrong number.	Yanlış numara.
What number do you want?	Hangi numarayı istiyorsunuz?
Can you connect me with 480606?	Bana 480606 numarayı bağlar mısınız?
Just a minute, please.	Bir dakika, lütfen.
Hold the line.	Ayrılmayınız.
Sorry, we were cut off.	Affedersiniz, hat kesildi.
You are through, now.	Konuşunuz şimdi, hat bağlandı.
Hello, who is speaking?	Alo, kimsiniz?

KEY TO PRONUNCIATION

c (jar), ç (church), g (gale), ğ (lengthen the preceding vowel), h (hill), ı (Cyril), j (Fr. *jeune*), ö (Fr. *peu* or Ger. *Köln*), s (sister), ş (shoe), ü (Fr. *dune* or Ger. *Glück*)

Is Miss ... available?	Bayan ... telefona gelebilir mi?
When will she be at home?	Saat kaçta evde olacak?
Do you expect her for lunch?	Öğle yemeğine bekliyor musunuz?
This is a personal call.	Özel olarak arıyorum.
No, there is no message.	Hayır, bir mesajım yok.
I will ring her again.	Tekrar ararım.
How much do I owe for the call?	Konuşma için borcum ne kadar?
Can you reverse the charge?	Karşı numaranın hesabına geçirebilir misiniz?
Give me six postcard stamps for Britain, airmail please.	Lütfen Britanyaya kartpostal için altı adet uçak pulu veriniz.
How much is it?	Ne kadar tutuyor?
When is the next collection?	Mektuplar ne zaman toplanıyor?
I want to send this telegram.	Bu telgrafı göndermek istiyorum.
It is an LT telegram.	Telgraf LT olacak.
I forgot to write my name and address.	Adımı ve adresimi yazmağı unuttum.
I want this to be an express telegram.	Bu telgrafın ekspres olarak gitmesini istiyorum.
Isn't there a reduced schedule operative on Sundays?	Pazar günleri için ucuz tarife yok mu?
I want to send a telegram with pre-paid reply.	Cevabı ödemeli bir tel çekmek istiyorum.
Thank you for your help.	Yardımınıza teşekkür ederim.

Chemist – Barber – Hairdresser

antiseptic	antiseptik	cologne	kolonya
aspirin	aspirin	comb	tarak
brilliantine	briyantin	cosmetics	makyaj malzemesi, kozmetik
brush	fırça		
colour rinse	benzer rengi tutturan saç boyası	cotton-wool	pamuk
		cream (cosmetic)	makyaj kremi
cold cream	yağlı krem		

KEY TO PRONUNCIATION

c (jar), ç (church), g (gale), ğ (lengthen the preceding vowel), h (hill), ı (Cyril), j (Fr. *jeune*), ö (Fr. *peu* or Ger. *Köln*), s (sister), ş (shoe), ü (Fr. *dune* or Ger. Glück)

Shopping

cough sweets	öksürük pastilleri	medicine	ilâç
cuticle cream	tırnak kremi	mouth-wash	ağız çalkalama ilâcı
denture cleaner	takma diş temizleyicisi	nail	tırnak
		nail brush	tırnak fırçası
deodorants	deodoran, ter ilacı	nail file	tırnak törpüsü
		nail scissors	tırnak makası
detergent	deterjan	nail varnish	tırnak cilâsı
disinfectant	dezenfektan	night cream	gece kremi
dry shampoo	kuru şampuan	ointment	merhem
dryer	saç kurutucusu, fö	parting	ayrık, ayırma
		perfume	parföm
dye, to	saç boyamak	permanent wave	permanent, perma
dye	saç boyası		
eyebrow pencil	kaş kalemi	prescription	reçete
eye shadow	far	powder	pudra
foundation cream	fon dö ten	powder-puff	pudra ponponu
		razor blade	tıraş bıçağı, jilet
gargle	gargara		
hair	saç	rollers	yuvarlak bigudi
hair bleach	peroksit	rouge	allık
hair cream	saç kremi	sanitary towels	femil, âdet bezi
hair curler	bigudi	shampoo	şampuan
hair fixative	saç sertleştiren ilâç	shaving brush	tıraş fırçası
		shaving cream	tıraş kremi
hair grip	toka	shaving soap	tıraş sabunu
hair lacquer	spray	shaving lotion	traş losyonu
hair lotion	saç losyonu	sleeping pill	uyku hapı
hair pins	firkete	soap	sabun
hair tint	hafif saç boyası	sticking plaster	plaster
laxative	müshil	sunglasses	güneş gözlüğü
lipstick	dudak boyası, ruj	suntan cream	güneş kremi
		talcum powder	talk pudrası
lotion	losyon	toilet paper	tuvalet kâğıdı
mascara	rimel	toilet soap	lüks sabun

KEY TO PRONUNCIATION

c (jar), ç (church), g (gale), ğ (lengthen the preceding vowel), h (hill), ı (Cyril), j (Fr. *jeune*), ö (Fr. *peu* or Ger. *Köln*), s (sister), ş (shoe), ü (Fr. *dune* or Ger. *Glück*)

tooth brush	diş fırçası	wave	dalga, saç kıvrımı
tooth paste	diş macunu		
vitamin cream	vitaminli krem	wave set	mizampli

Phrases

Is there a barber shop near here?	Civarda bir berber dükkânı bulunur mu?
How far is the hairdresser from here?	Kadın berberi buradan ne kadar uzakta?
At what time do they open?	Saat kaçta açıyorlar?
At what time does the hairdresser close?	Kadın berberi kaçta kapıyor?
Do I have to have an appointment?	Randevu almam lazım mı?
I want a haircut, please.	Saçımı kestirmek istiyorum.
I want a shave.	Traş olmak istiyorum!
I want my hair trimmed, please.	Sadece saçımı düzeltiniz, lütfen.
Please don't cut it short.	Lütfen kısa kesmeyiniz.
I would like it short at the back.	Arkasını kısa kesiniz.
Do not cut my whiskers.	Yanlarını (favorilerimi) kesmeyiniz.
Don't put anything on my hair.	Saçıma bir şey sürmeyiniz.
Comb it with water, please.	Suyla tarayınız lütfen.
I want my nails manicured.	Tırnaklarıma manikür istiyorum.
Have you anyone here for pedicure?	Burada pedikür yapacak kimse bulunur mu?
I want a shampoo and set.	Şampuan ve mizampli istiyorum.
How long does one wait for a perm?	Permenant için ne kadar beklenir?
I want a colour rinse.	Hafif saç boyası istiyorum.
I should like to try a new style of hairdressing.	Yeni bir saç stili denemek istiyorum.
Would you please set my hair with rollers?	Saçımı yuvarlak bigudilerle sarabilir misiniz?
Do it without rollers, please.	Lütfen bigudi kullanmayınız.
Would you wash my hair?	Saçımı yıkar mısınız?

KEY TO PRONUNCIATION

c (jar), ç (church), g (gale), ğ (lengthen the preceding vowel), h (hill), ı (Cyril), j (Fr. *jeune*), ö (Fr. *peu* or Ger. *Köln*), s (sister), ş (shoe), ü (Fr. *dune* or Ger. *Glück*)

Shopping

The water is too hot.	Su çok sıcak.
The dryer is too hot, can you adjust it?	Saç kurutucu çok kızmış, ayarlayabilir misiniz?
My hair is dry.	Saçım kuru.
I would like some cream.	Saç kremi istiyorum.
I would like some hair oil.	Saç yağı (briyantin) istiyorum.
I don't want a hot towel for my face.	Yüzüm için sıcak havlu istemiyorum.
How much do I have to pay?	Borcum ne kadar?
Is the tip included?	Bahşıs dahil mi?
I wanted to buy some scent.	Parföm satın alacaktım.
Do you sell lipstick?	Dudak boyası satıyor musunuz?
Do you sell a hair restorer?	Dökülen saçların çıkmasına yardım edecek bir ilâcınız var mı?

At the chemist's

I want some Aspros (aspirins).	Aspro (aspirin) istiyorum.
Can I buy it without a prescription?	Reçetesiz satın alabilir miyim?
Can you make this prescription, please?	Bu reçeteyi lütfen yapar mısınız?
Does it matter if it is a foreign prescription?	Yabancı reçete olmasının mahzuru var mı?
Please give me something for	Lütfen bana
— diarrhoea.	— amel
— indigestion.	—hazımsızlık
— toothache.	—dişağrısı
— sea-sickness.	— deniz tutması için bir sey verebilir misiniz?
Have you got anything for sunburn?	Güneş yanması için bir ilâcınız var mı?
Have you something to soothe the pain?	Acısını alacak bir şeyiniz bulunur mu?
How does one take it?	Nasıl alınıyor?
How often should I take it?	Ne kadar sık almam gerekir?

KEY TO PRONUNCIATION

c (jar), ç (church), g (gale), ğ (lengthen the preceding vowel), h (hill), ı (Cyril), j (Fr. *jeune*), ö (Fr. *peu* or Ger. *Köln*), s (sister), ş (shoe), ü (Fr. *dune* or Ger. Glück)

Take twice a day after meals.	Günde iki defa yemeklerden sonra.
— before meals.	— yemeklerden önce alınız.
Take one every four hours.	Her dört saatte bir tane alınız.
How do I drink this syrup?	Bu şurubu nasıl içeyim?
Will a teaspoonful do?	Bir çay kaşığı yeter mi?
Please use a table-spoon and drink whenever you start coughing.	Lütfen bir yemek kaşığı kullanınız ve öksürük başlar başlamaz içiniz.
Can you recommend a gargle?	Bir gargara tavsiye eder misiniz?
I have cut my hand.	Elimi kestim.
Could you give me some cotton wool?	Pamuk verebilir misiniz?
Have you got something to stop it bleeding?	Kanı durduracak bir şeyiniz var mı?
Can you dress this wound?	Bu yarayı bandaj yapar mısınız?
Can you give something for an insect bite?	Böcek sokmasına karşı bir şey verebilir misiniz?
I need some sleeping pills.	Uyku ilâcı istiyorum.
Please give me something to stop my diarrhoea.	Lütfen amelimi dindirecek bir ilâç veriniz.

Photography

Tourists are usually free to take photographs or shoot films in museums, mosques or churches in Turkey. The fee is twice the fee charged for entrance. Professional photographers, shooting films or taking photographs for commercial purposes, have to obtain official permission from the authorities concerned. The use of tripod and flashes are subject to permission from the administration of the museum, mosque or church in question.

One of the customs to be conformed with is the removal of shoes when entering a mosque. Usually, the doorkeeper offers tourists large slippers at the entrance which they put on to cover their shoes or they remove their shoes and walk in their stockings. The floor of the mosque is covered with carpets upon which people put their foreheads during prayer, hence Moslems take off their shoes and enter the holy place with bare feet. In the mosque, tourists are expected to speak quietly and not go pushing about between rows of worshippers.

KEY TO PRONUNCIATION

c (jar), ç (church), g (gale), ğ (lengthen the preceding vowel), h (hill), ı (Cyril), j (Fr. *jeune*), ö (Fr. *peu* or Ger. *Köln*), s (sister), ş (shoe), ü (Fr. *dune* or Ger. Gülck)

Shopping

In a country with such a fascinating historical background as Turkey, it is natural that there are many museums. Most towns and cities have at least one. Istanbul has more than ten. Most museums in Istanbul are closed on Mondays.

Vocabulary

camera	fotograf makinesi	lens-hood	adese kapağı, objektif dış kapağı
card	kart	light meter	ışık ölçeği
case	kutu, mahfaza	matt	mat
cine-camera	film makinesi	micro-film	mikrofilm
colour film	renkli film	negative	negatif
develop, to	develope etmek, yıkatmak	print	negatiften yapılan kopye
enlarge, to	agrandizman yaptırmak, büyütmek	print, to	camdan kağıda kopye basmak
enlarged print	agrandizman	range-finder	mesafe ölçen
exposed	fazla ekspoze edilmiş, çok ışık almış	shutter	objektif kapağı
		slide	slayd, diyapozitif
		size	büyüklük
		snapshot	enstantane
film	fotograf filmi, sinema filmi	spool	makara
		tripod	fotograf makinesi ayağı
film winder	film sarıcı		
filter	filtre	television film	televizyon filmi
flash bulb	flaş ampulü		
glossy	parlak	under-exposed	tam ışık almamış, iyi ekspoze edilmemiş
lens	adese, objektif		

Phrases

I want a colour film.	Bir renkli film istiyorum.
What size do you want?	Ne büyüklükte istiyorsunuz?
I want a 36 pictured Kodachrome K.135–36p.	36 renkli slaydı olan Kodakrom film istiyorum.
Have you got the camera with you?	Fotograf makinesi yanınızda mı?

KEY TO PRONUNCIATION

c (jar), ç (church), g (gale), ğ (lengthen the preceding vowel), h (hill), ı (Cyril), j (Fr. *jeune*), ö (Fr. *peu* or Ger. *Köln*), s (sister), ş (shoe), ü (Fr. *dune* or Ger. *Glück*)

Here is my camera.	İşte fotoğraf makinem.
Have you Kodachrome II with only twenty slides?	Yalnız yirmi slaydlık Kodakrom II filminiz var mı?
Does the price include developing?	Fiatına banyo da dahil mi?
Will you develop this black and white film?	Bu siyah beyaz filmi develope eder misiniz?
I want a print of each.	Her birinden bir kopye istiyorum.
How much is it going to be?	Ne kadar tutacak?
I should like to have this photo enlarged.	Bu fotoğrafı büyütmek istiyorum.
What size would you like them?	Kopyeleri ne boy istiyorsunuz?
6 x 9 would do.	6 x 9 büyüklük işime yarar.
How much would an enlargement cost?	Agrandizman kaça olur?
Would you like any in postcard size?	Kartpostal büyüklüğünde istedikleriniz var mı?
No, I don't need that size.	Hayır, o boya lüzum yok.
When shall I call to collect them?	Ne zaman gelip alabilirim?
Will they be ready soon?	Çabuk hazır olur mu?
They are a bit under-exposed.	Film tam ekspoze edilmemiştir.
Will you please be careful when developing?	Filmi develope ederken, itina gösterir misiniz, lütfen?
The film is jammed.	Film takılmış, dönmüyor.
I can't turn the knob.	Makara kolunu çeviremiyorum.
Can it be repaired?	Tamir edilebilir mi?
How soon can you do it?	Ne kadar zamanda yapabilirsiniz?
How much will you charge for it?	Tamiri kaç para tutacak?
Do you have some flash-bulbs?	Flaş ampulu bulunur mu?
Have you a photo-album?	Fotoğraf için album bulunur mu?
Is there a Kodak processing laboratory in Turkey?	Türkiyede Kodak film laboratuvarı var mı?
Do colour films have to be sent abroad for processing?	Renkli filmlerin banyo edilmesi için yurtdışına gönderilmesi lazım mı?

KEY TO PRONUNCIATION

c (jar), ç (church), g (gale), ğ (lengthen the preceding vowel), h (hill), ı (Cyril), j (Fr. *jeune*), ö (Fr. *peu* or Ger. *Köln*), s (sister), ş (shoe), ü (Fr. *dune* or Ger. Glück)

14 Paying a visit and writing a letter

Vocabulary

address	adres	informal letter	özel mektup, resmi olmiyan
addressee	mektup gönderilen	ink	mürekkep
answer, to	cevap vermek	inkstand	hokka
appointment	randevu	introduce, to	takdim etmek, tanıştırmak
Biro	Biro, tükenmez		
blotting paper	papye buar	invitation	davet
business letter	iş mektubu	invite, to	davet etmek
carbon copy	kopye	invoice	fatura
carbon paper	karbon kâğıdı kopye kâğıdı	letter	mektup
		letter of condolence	tâziye mektubu
card index	fiş indeksi		
coloured pencil	boya kalemi renkli kalem	letter of congratulations	tebrik mektubu
conversation	konuşma	letter of sympathy	başsağlığı mektubu
copy, to	kopye çıkarmak		
copybook	defter	letter-file	mektup dosyası
envelope	zarf	pad	blok, kâğıt destesi
express letter	ekspres mektup,		
formal letter	resmi mektup	paper	kâğıt
fountain pen	dolmakalem	party	parti
glue	tutkal	pen	yazıkalemi
gum	zamk	pencil	kurşunkalem
handwriting	elyazısı	personal letter	şahsi mektup
heading	başlık	postcard	kartpostal

KEY TO PRONUNCIATION

c (jar), ç (church), g (gale), ğ (lengthen the preceding vowel), h (hill), ı (Cyril), j (Fr. *jeune*), ö (Fr. *peu* or Ger. *Köln*), s (sister), ş (shoe), ü (Fr. *dune* or Ger. Glück)

Paying a visit and writing a letter

reception	resepsiyon, kabul resmi	stick, to	tutturmak, yapıştırmak
ring the bell, to	zili çalmak	talk, to	konuşmak
rubber	lastik, silgi	type, to	daktilo etmek
seal, to	yapıştırmak, mühürlemek	typewriter	yazı makinesi
		urgent letter	acele mektup
sealing wax	mühür mumu	visit	ziyaret
send, to	göndermek	visit, to	ziyaret etmek
sender	mektubu gönderen	visiting-card	kartvizit
		write, to	yazmak
shorthand	steno	writing-desk	yazı masası
signature	imza	writing paper	yazı kâğıdı
stationery	kırtasiye	writing-pad	bloknot

Paying a visit – Phrases

Is Mrs. Gül at home?	Bayan Gül evde mi?
She had asked me to call on her today.	Bugün kendisini ziyaret etmemi söylemişti.
Yes, I am invited.	Evet, dâvetliyim.
Do come in, please!	Lütfen, içeri buyrunuz!
It was nice of you to accept my invitation.	Dâvetimi kabul etmiş olmanıza çok sevindim.
I am very pleased to see you!	Sizi gördüğüme çok sevindim!
Thank you for your invitation.	Davetinize teşekkür ederim.
It was kind of you to ask me!	Beni çağırmakla nezaket gösterdiniz!
This is my sister.	Kızkardeşim.
May I introduce my husband?	Kocamı takdim edebilir miyim?
I want you to meet my friend.	Arkadaşımı tanıştırmak isterim.
It is a great pleasure to me.	Benim için büyük bir zevk olur.
The pleasure is mine!	O zevk bana ait!
Won't you stay to lunch?	Öğle yemeğine kalmaz mısınız?
Are you free this evening?	Bu akşam boş musunuz?
How about going to a theatre with me?	Benimle tiyatroya gitmeğe ne dersiniz?

KEY TO PRONUNCIATION

c (jar), ç (church), g (gale), ğ (lengthen the preceding vowel), h (hill), ı (Cyril), j (Fr. *jeune*), ö (Fr. *peu* or Ger. *Köln*), s (sister), ş (shoe), ü (Fr. *dune* or Ger. Glück)

Paying a visit and writing a letter

I wish you could stay a little longer.	Keşke bir parça daha kalabilseniz.
We are sorry, but we have to go.	Maalesef, gitmemiz lazım.
Next time we shall stay longer.	Gelecek sefer daha uzun kalırız.
Let us have tea together.	Beraber bir çay içelim.
Many thanks for your hospitality!	Gösterdiğiniz misafirperverliğe çok teşekkür ederiz!
Where shall we meet tomorrow?	Yarın nerede buluşalım?
Would you meet me at the Divan Hotel?	Divan Otelinde beni bekler misiniz?
Same place, same time!	Herzamanki yerde ve herzamanki saatte!
Remember me to your parents.	Annenize babanıza hürmetler.
See you soon!	Yakında görüşmek üzere!

Writing a letter – Phrases

I want to write a letter.	Bir mektup yazmak istiyorum.
Would you please give some paper?	Bana biraz kâğıt verebilir misiniz?
I need an envelope.	Bana bir zarf lazım.
There are envelopes and paper on the desk.	Yazı masasında kâğıt ve zarf var.
Do you have a selection of postcards?	Çeşitli kartpostallarınız var mı?
I have to write an urgent letter!	Çok acele bir mektup yazmam lazım!
Is there a typewriter that I can use?	Kullanabileceğim bir yazı makinesi var mı?
Can you type it for me?	Bana daktilo edebilir misiniz?
I have run out of ink.	Mürekkebim bitmiş!
Could I borrow your fountain pen?	Dolmakaleminizi ödünç alabilir miydim?
I have to answer some letters.	Mektuplara cevap yazmam lazım.
Can she take it down in shorthand?	Sekreteriniz stenoyla not edebilir mi?

KEY TO PRONUNCIATION
c (jar), ç (church), g (gale), ğ (lengthen the preceding vowel), h (hill), ı (Cyril), j (Fr. *jeune*), ö (Fr. *peu* or Ger. *Köln*), s (sister), ş (shoe), ü (Fr. *dune* or Ger. *Glück*)

Paying a visit and writing a letter

Can she make a carbon copy for me?	Benim için bir kopye çıkartabilir mi?
Dear Sir,	Sayın Bay,
Dear Sirs,	Sayın Baylar,
Dear Madam,	Sayın Bayan,
Dear Professor,	Sayın Profesör,
Dear Mrs. Gül,	Sayın Bayan Gül,
Dear Mr. Demir,	Sayın Bay Demir,
Gentlemen,	Sayın Baylar,
In reply to your letter ...	... mektubunuza cevaben
I have received your letter of 12 November.	12 Kasım tarihli mektubunuzu aldım.
You have not answered my letter.	Mektubuma cevap alamadım.
I should like to advise you.	Size bildirmek isterim.
I beg to inform you that ...	... i bilginize sunarım.
I shall be glad if you would ...	... yaparsanız memnun olurum.
I acknowledge the receipt of your letter.	Mektubunuzu aldığımı bildiririm.
It was indeed a pleasure to receive your letter.	Mektubunuzu almak gerçekten bana bir zevk oldu.
Thank you for your kind letter.	Nazik mektubunuza teşekkür ederim.
I had great pleasure in reading your letter.	Mektubunuzu okumaktan büyük bir zevk duydum.
Please accept my deepest sympathy!	En derin tâziyelerimi lütfen kabul buyurunuz!
I should like to express my sincere condolences!	Samimi tâziyelerimi ifade etmek isterim!
I was very pleased to hear the news of your marriage.	Evlenme haberinizi duymakla çok memnun oldum.
I wish you a very happy birthday!	Size mutlu bir doğum günü dilerim!
Many happy returns!	Nice senelere!
Congratulations on your engagement!	Nişanınızı tebrik ederim!

KEY TO PRONUNCIATION

c (jar), ç (church), g (gale), ğ (lengthen the preceding vowel), h (hill), ı (Cyril), j (Fr. *jeune*), ö (Fr. *peu* or Ger. *Köln*), s (sister), ş (shoe), ü (Fr. *dune* or Ger. *Glück*)

Paying a visit and writing a letter 123

Thank you very much for your kind invitation to cocktails.	Kokteyl için nazik dâvetinize çok teşekkür ederim.
— to dinner.	Akşam yemeği için.
— to lunch.	Öğle yemeği için.
I shall be pleased to accept it.	Kabul etmek benim için bir şeref olur.
I regret not to be able to accept it, as I shall be leaving tomorrow. Thank you for asking me all the same.	Kabul edemiyeceğim için özür dilerim, yarın ayrılıyorum. Davet lütfünüze yine de teşekkür ederim.
With best wishes,	En iyi dileklerimle,
With kind regards,	Derin hürmetlerimle,
Yours faithfully,	Saygılarla,
Yours sincerely,	(Sevgi ve) saygılarımla,

A business letter   *Bir iş mektubu*

The Manager, Hotel Grand Ephesus, İzmir, Turkey.	Büyük Efes Oteli Müdürlüğüne, İzmir, Türkiye.
Dear Sir,	Sayın Bay,
I shall be glad if you would reserve me a single room with a bath, overlooking the sea, for the week starting 17 May.	17 Mayıs tarihinde başlıyan hafta için, bana tek yataklı, banyolu ve denize bakan bir oda ayırmanızı reca edeceğim.
I shall look forward to receiving your confirmation of this booking at your earliest convenience. Thanking you in anticipation,	İlk fırsatta rezervasyonu teyid eden mektubunuzu bekler, teşekkürlerimi sunarım.
Yours faithfully,	Saygılarla,

An Application for a Licence   *Bir Dilekçe*

Head of the Administrative District of Çankaya, Çankaya, Ankara.	Çankaya Kaymakamlığına Çankaya, Ankara.

KEY TO PRONUNCIATION

c (jar), ç (church), g (gale), ğ (lengthen the preceding vowel), h (hill), ı (Cyril), j (Fr. *jeune*), ö (Fr. *peu* or Ger. *Köln*), s (sister), ş (shoe), ü (Fr. *dune* or Ger. *Glück*

I*

I am a member of the Ankara
Avcılar ve Atçılar Kulübü.
I should like to go hunting in
this region.
I shall be much obliged if you
would provide me with a hunting
licence.
I have pleasure in submitting
the relevant information.

Ankara Avcılar ve Atçılar
Kulübü üyesiyim.
Bu civarda ava çıkmak
istiyorum.
Bu münasebetle bir av
tezkeresi düzenlenerek
verilmesini reca ederim.
Gerekli bilgi saygiyle
sunulmuştur.

Christian and surname
Father's full name
Date and place of birth
Nationality
Occupation
Address in Ankara
Passport number

Adı, Soyadı
Baba adı
Doğum yılı ve yeri
Uyruğu
Işi
Ankara adresi
Pasaport numarası

An informal letter of invitation

My dear Mrs. Gül,
I am writing you these lines to
request the pleasure of your and
your husband's company at a
cocktail party we are giving on
Saturday next at our hotel.
Looking forward to hearing
from you and with kind regards,
Yours sincerely,

Bir davet mektubu

Sevgili Bayan Gül,
Gelecek Cumartesi otelimizde
tertiplediğimiz kokteyle eşinizle
birlikte şeref vermenizi dilemek
için bu satırları yazıyorum.

Cevabınızı bekler, sevgi ve
saygılarımı sunarım.

An acceptance

My dear Mrs. Wilson,
Thank you for your kind letter.
We shall be very pleased to accept
your invitation for cocktails on
Saturday next at your hotel.
Looking forward to seeing you
both soon,
Yours sincerely,

Davetin kabulü

Sevgili Bayan Wilson,
Nazik mektubunuza teşekkür
ederim. Önümüzdeki Cumartesi
otelinizde vereceğiniz kokteyl
için vaki davetinizi memnuniyetle
kabul ettiğimizi bildirir, pek
yakında görüşmek emeliyle,
sevgi ve saygılarımı sunarım.

KEY TO PRONUNCIATION

c (jar), ç (church), g (gale), ğ (lengthen the preceding vowel), h (hill), ı (Cyril),
j (Fr. *jeune*), ö (Fr. *peu* or Ger. *Köln*), s (sister), ş (shoe), ü (Fr. *dune* or Ger.
Glück)

Regrets

My dear Mrs. Wilson,

We should like to thank you for your kind invitation. It would have been indeed a great pleasure for us to be there. Unfortunately, we have already promised to be with ...'s over the weekend, and so are unable to accept. However, I shall call on you on our return. Thanking you again for asking us.

Yours sincerely,

A letter of thanks

My dear Miss Arda,

It was very kind of you to think of us at Christmas. I was delighted to receive the parcel bringing me a box of Turkish Delight and a silver pin bearing the Sultan's signature.

I have enjoyed telling my friends about our stay in your unforgettable country, Turkey.

I want to thank you for giving me something so lovely to remember you by.

My husband joins me in sending our best wishes for the New Year.

Yours sincerely,

İtizar

Sevgili Bayan Wilson,

Nazik davetinize teşekkür etmek isteriz. Orada bulunmak her ikimiz icin de büyük bir zevk olurdu. Ancak, hafta sonunu ...' larla geçirmek üzere söz vermiş bulunuyoruz, bu sebepten, maalesef davetinizi kabul edemiyeceğimiz için bizi mazur görünüz. Dönüşümüzde sizi ararım. Davetiniz için tekrar teşekkür ederek, sevgi ve saygılarımla,

Bir teşekkür mektubu

Sevgili Bayan Arda,

Bizleri Noel'de düşünmek nezaketinize çok duygulandık. Lokum kutusuyla, gümüş tuğralı iğneyi getiren paketi almak beni son derece sevindirdi.

Unutulmaz memleketiniz Türkiyede geçirdiğimiz günleri dostlarıma anlata anlata bitiremedim.

Sizi daima hatırlatacak böyle sevimli bir hediye verdiğiniz için candan teşekkür etmek isterim.

Eşimle birlikte Yeni Yıl için en iyi dileklerimizi sunarız.

Sonsuz sevgilerimle,

KEY TO PRONUNCIATION

c (jar), ç (church), g (gale), ğ (lengthen the preceding vowel), h (hill), ı (Cyril), j (Fr. *jeune*), ö (Fr. *peu* or Ger. *Köln*), s (sister), ş (shoe), ü (Fr. *dune* or Ger. *Glück*)

15 Recreation

Sports

ATHLETICS	ATLETİZM	FOOTBALL	FUTBOL
athletics	atletizm	team	takım
meetings	yarışmaları	ball	top
cross country	kroskantri	game	oyun
run	koşusu	match	maç
discus throw	disk atışı	goal	gol
high jump	yüksek	goal-kick	avut atışı
	atlama	free kick	frikik, ceza
hurdles	manialı koşu		atışı
triple	üç adım	handball	hendbol
jump	atlama	opponent	hasım
long jump	uzun atlama	penalty	penaltı
javelin	cirit	play, to	oynamak
pole vault	sırıkla atlama	player	oyuncu
shot put	gülle atma	pitch	saha
relay race	bayrak yarışı	referee	hakem
BOATING	KÜREK ÇEKMEK, YELKEN AÇMAK	touch throw	taç atışı
		GOLFING	GOLF OYUNU
BOXING	BOKS	HORSE RACING	AT YARIŞI
BICYCLING	BİSİKLETE BİNME	bet	bahis
		favourite	favori
FENCING	ESKRİM- CİLİK	horse	at
		jockey	cokey

KEY TO PRONUNCIATION

c (jar), ç (church), g (gale), ğ (lengthen the preceding vowel), h (hill), ı (Cyril), j (Fr. *jeune*), ö (Fr. *peu* or Ger. *Köln*), s (sister), ş (shoe), ü (Fr. *dune* or Ger. Glück)

Recreation

photo-finish	fotofiniş	SWIMMING	YÜZME
place	plase	dive, to	dalmak
race course	koşu alanı	swim, to	yüzmek
tote	müşterek-bahis	swimming pool	yüzme havuzu
HORSEBACK-RIDING	BİNİCİLİK	underwater swimming	sualtında yüzme
ROWING	KÜREK ÇEKMEK	TENNIS	TENİS
		singles	tek
SKATING	PATİNAJ YAPMAK	doubles	çift
		racket	raket
SKIING	KAYAK YAPMAK, KAYAKÇILIK	score	yapılan sayı
		tennis ball	tenis topu
		tennis shoes	tenis ayakkabısı
ski-lift	ski asansörü		
WATER SKIING	SUDA KAYAK YAPMAK	net	ağ
		WRESTLING	GÜREŞ
		oil wrestling	yağlı güreş
SPORTS-GROUND	SPOR ALANI	free-style wrestling	serbes güreş
		Greco-Roman wrestling	Grekoromen güreş

Games – Vocabulary

backgammon	tavla	king	papas
billiards	bilardo	knave	oğlan, bacak
billiard table	bilardo masası	no-trump	kozsuz
billiard cue	isteka	pack of cards	ıskambil kâğıdı
bridge	briç		
ace	as, birli	queen	kız
cards	kâğıtlar	spades	karamaça, maça
clubs	sinek, trefl		
diamonds	karo	slam	şilem
down	aşağı	trump	koz
down, to be	aşağı düşmek	vulnerable	zonda olmak
game	oyun	zone	zon
hearts	kupa, kör		

KEY TO PRONUNCIATION

c (jar), ç (church), g (gale), ğ (lengthen the preceding vowel), h (hill), ı (Cyril), j (Fr. *jeune*), ö (Fr. *peu* or Ger. *Köln*), s (sister), ş (shoe), ü (Fr. *dune* or Ger. Glück)

chess	satranç	draughts	dama
dice	zar	table tennis	ping pong, masa tenisi
dominoes	domino		

Entertainments – Vocabulary

ball	balo	funfair	lunapark
band	bando	gambling	kumar oynamak
box (theatre)	loca	interval	ara
box-office	gişe	night-club	bar, gece kulübü
casino	kumar oynanan yer	opera	opera
cinema	sinema	orchestra	orkestra
circle	balkon	pit	sinema salonu alt katı
cloakroom	gardrop		
cloakroom ticket	gardrop bileti	play	piyes
comedy	komedi	revue	rövü
concert	konser	seat	oturacak yer
concert-hall	konser salonu	show	şov, varyete
dance	dans	stage	sahne
dance, to	dans etmek	stalls	koltuk
dancer	dansör, dansöz	theatre	tiyatro
dress circle	lüks balkon	tragedy	trajedi
entertainment	eğlence	upper circle	galeri, üst balkon
fair	fuar		
fancy dress ball	maskeli balo	usherette	yer gösteren kız
festival	festival	variety show	varyete oyunları
film	film	vaudeville	vodvil
folk dance	halkoyunu	ventriloquist	vantrilok

Phrases

Where can I find a rowing boat for hire?	Kiralık sandal nerede bulabilirim?
I want to hire a motor boat.	Bir motör kiralamak istiyorum.
I want to go sailing.	Yelkenliyle gezmek istiyorum.
I want to go swimming.	Yüzmek istiyorum.

KEY TO PRONUNCIATION

c (jar), ç (church), g (gale), ğ (lengthen the preceding vowel), h (hill), ı (Cyril), j (Fr. *jeune*), ö (Fr. *peu* or Ger. *Köln*), s (sister), ş (shoe), ü (Fr. *dune* or Ger. Glück)

Recreation

Is it deep here?	Burası derin mi?
Can I dive here?	Buradan dalabilir miyim?
Is the sea deep over there?	Orada deniz derin mi?
How is it? Is it very deep?	Nasıl, derin mi çok?
Are there rocks?	Kayalık mı?
Is there sea-weed?	Yosun var mı?
I cannot swim very well.	İyi yüzemiyorum.
Can you swim on your back?	Arkaüstü yüzebilir misin?
Is the water cold?	Su soğuk mu?
No, it's lovely!	Hayır, çok güzel!
I have got a cramp!	Kramp girdi!
Please help me ashore!	Denizden çıkmama yardım edin, lütfen!
Don't swim beyond the buoys.	Şamandıralardan dışarı yüzmeyiniz.
Are there many fish here?	Burada çok balık var mı?
Where is the best place for fish?	Balık avlamak için en iyi yer neresi?
It is terribly hot!	Son derece sıcak var!
Can one hire a towel?	Havlu kiralanabilir mi?
My friends and I should like to go rowing.	Arkadaşlarımla birlikte kürek çekmek istiyoruz.
Is the sea rough for rowing?	Kürek çekmek için deniz çok mu dalgalı?
The boat has sprung a leak!	Sandal su alıyor!
Are you going to the races?	At yarışlarına gidiyor musunuz?
How do we get there?	Oraya nasıl gidilir?
Which is the favourite?	Favori hangisi?
Where can one see wrestling?	Nerede güreş seyredilebilir?
Is there a wrestling match tonight?	Bu gece bir güreş yarışması var mı?
We should like to go to a football match.	Bir futbol maçına gitmek istiyoruz.
Which match do you recommend?	Hangi maçı tavsiye edersiniz?
Is it an international match?	Milli maç mı?

KEY TO PRONUNCIATION

c (jar), ç (church), g (gale), ğ (lengthen the preceding vowel), h (hill), ı (Cyril), j (Fr. *jeune*), ö (Fr. *peu* or Ger. *Köln*), s (sister), ş (shoe), ü (Fr. *dune* or Ger. *Glück*)

Recreation

Would you care for a game of bridge?	Briç oynar mısınız?
Where does one play poker here?	Burada poker nerede oynanıyor?
We want to see a film.	Film seyretmek istiyoruz.
Do you know what is on at the cinema?	Sinemada acaba ne oynuyor?
Who is playing in it?	Oyniyanlar kim?
Should we book seats?	Önceden yer kapatmak lazım mı?
Is the film in Turkish?	Film Türkçe sözlü mü?
Would you like to come with us?	Bizimle gelmek ister misiniz?
Two balcony seats for tonight.	Bu akşam için iki balkon.
Show me where they are on the plan.	Planda yerlerini gösterebilir misiniz?
Do you know what is on at the theatre?	Tiyatroda acaba ne oynuyor?
I should love to see the Janissary Band!	Mehter Takımını çok görmek istiyorum!
Where do they perform?	Nerede çalıyorlar?
Shall we go dancing?	Dansa gidelim mi?
Would you care to dance?	Dans eder misiniz?
I don't know how to dance this one.	Bunu dansetmesini bilmiyorum.
Is there a tennis court near here?	Bu civarda bir tenis kortu var mı?
My wife and I play tennis.	Eşimle ben tenis oynarız.
Shall we play cards?	Iskambil oyniyalım mı?
Have you got a new pack?	Yeni bir deste var mı?
I have shuffled it.	Ben karıştırdım!
It is your turn to cut.	Kesmek sırası sende.
Don't look at my cards!	Elimdeki kağıtlara bakmayınız!
Is there a riding school here?	Burada Binicilik okulu var mı?
I should like to take some riding lessons.	Ata binme dersleri almak istiyorum.
Where is the nearest golf-course?	En yakın golf sahası nerede?
Can I play golf without becoming a member?	Üye olmadan golf oyniyabilir miyim?

KEY TO PRONUNCIATION

c (jar), ç (church), g (gale), ğ (lengthen the preceding vowel), h (hill), ı (Cyril), j (Fr. *jeune*), ö (Fr. *peu* or Ger. *Köln*), s (sister), ş (shoe), ü (Fr. *dune* or Ger. Glück)

16 Sightseeing

Vocabulary

Aergus	Erciyaş	design	desen, şekil
ancient site	eski yer, tarihi saha	Didymi	Didime
		Ephesus	Efes, Selçuk
Anno Domini	Milâttan sonra	epoch	çağ, devir
Antioch	Antakya	fortress	hisar, kala
aqueduct	su kemeri	gallery	galeri
arch	kemer	garden	bahçe
Asia Minor	Anadolu, Küçük Asya	gate	kapı
		grave	mezar
Aspendos	Aspendos, Belkız	guide	rehber, kılavuz
Attalea	Antalya	Hellenistic	Helenistik
battlement	kale dıvarı gibi mazgallı	icon	ikon, aziz resmi veya heykeli
Before Christ	Milâttan önce	Iconium	Konya
Bosphorus	Boğaziçi	inscription	yazı, kitabe
bridge	köprü	interpreter	tercüman
building	bina	Lycia	Likya, Muğla dolayları
carving	oyma		
Caesarea	Kayseri	Mausoleum	Mozole, Kabir, Anıtkabir
castle	kala, şato		
cathedral	katedral	monument	anıt
century	yüzyıl, asır	mosque	cami
church	kilise	mosaic	mozaik
Cilicia	Kilikya, Adana dolayları	museum	müze
		Mysia	Misya, Çanakkale dolayları
cistern	sarnıç		
column	sütun	palace	saray

KEY TO PRONUNCIATION

c (jar), ç (church), g (gale), ğ (lengthen the preceding vowel), h (hill), ı (Cyril), j (Fr. *jeune*), ö (Fr. *peu* or Ger. *Köln*), s (sister), ş (shoe), ü (Fr. *dune* or Ger. *Glück*)

park	park	statue	heykel
Pergamum	Bergama	style	stil, uslup
Perge	Perge	Taurus mountains	Toros dağları
pot	kap, kavanoz		
pots and pans	çanak çömlek	temple	mabet, tapınak
prehistoric	tarihten önce, tarih öncesi	theatre	tiyatro
		tile	çini
Princes Isles	Adalar	tomb	mezar, kabir
Roman	Romalı, Romalılara ait	Troy	Truva
		Turkish	Türk
ruin	harabe	vase	vazo
street	yol, cadde	wall	dıvar, sur
street-plan	yol planı	Whirling Dervishes	Mevlevi dervişleri
square	meydan		
stadium	stadyum		

Visiting Turkish baths

Turkish baths or *Hamam* as they are called in Turkey, were originated to comply with one of the requirements of Islam, cleanliness. Unlike *savunas*, they are not intended for weight reduction.

In a Turkish bath water is conveyed through earthenware pipes, collected in a reservoir, boiled, and poured over the body from a copper bowl filled at a tap. When the body perspires, it is rubbed with a hair glove to open the pores.

In Turkey, there are baths for men, for women, and those with mixed but separate facilities. There are also many thousands of baths built on a smaller scale in private homes.

Public baths of this nature are scattered throughout the country. In Istanbul, İzmir, Ankara and Bursa there are hundreds of Turkish baths. The oldest and most picturesque *hamam* in Ankara is Karacabey, a fifteenth-century Turkish bath. In Turkish baths, one used to relax, be scoured with a rough cloth or pounded by a masseur (*tellâk*) and have tea or sandwiches served up in a dressing room. In Ottoman times, women would spend the entire day at a bath, taking their food with them and amusing themselves with gossip, games and music.

KEY TO PRONUNCIATION

c (jar), ç (church), g (gale), ğ (lengthen the preceding vowel), h (hill), ı (Cyril), j (Fr. *jeune*), ö (Fr. *peu* or Ger. *Köln*), s (sister), ş (shoe), ü (Fr. *dune* or Ger. Glück)

Sightseeing

It is customary to walk on the heated marble floor of the bath wearing wooden raised clogs, and wrapped in a large towel or *bornoz*.

Baths are open every day from 6 p.m. to 10 p.m., unless otherwise announced.

Phrases

Do you have a list of sightseeing tours?	Gezinti turlarına ait bir program var mı?
Are the tours by coach or by car?	Turlar otobüsle mi, otomobille mi?
How much is the sightseeing tour?	Gezinti turu kaç paraya?
Are entrance fees included in the price?	Girişler fiata dahil mi?
Is it a half-day tour?	Yarım günlük bir gezi mi?
Is it a whole-day tour?	Bütün günlük bir gezi mi?
Is lunch included on a full-day tour?	Bir günlük gezi fiatına öğle yemeği dahil mi?
Does the price include the services of a guide?	Fiata rehber ücreti de dahil mi?
Please give me two tickets on your half day excursion to ...	Lütfen ...'e yarım günlük gezinti için iki yer istiyorum.
We should like to be on the same coach.	Aynı otobüste olmak istiyoruz.
I want to go sightseeing by myself.	Kendi başıma gezintiye çıkmak istiyorum.
I want to have a guide who speaks English.	İngilizce konuşan bir rehber istiyorum.
How much should one pay the guide?	Rehbere kaç para ödemek lazım?
Where does one take a boat to the Bosphorus?	Boğaziçi vapuruna nereden binilir?
Where does one take the ferry for the Princes Isles?	Adalar vapuruna nereden binilir?
Where can I get the tickets?	Biletleri nereden alabilirim?
Do you have to queue?	Kuyruğa girmek lazım mı?

KEY TO PRONUNCIATION

c (jar), ç (church), g (gale), ğ (lengthen the preceding vowel), h (hill), ı (Cyril), j (Fr. *jeune*), ö (Fr. *peu* or Ger. *Köln*), s (sister), ş (shoe), ü (Fr. *dune* or Ger. *Glück*)

How long does it take to the Princes Isles?	Adalara gitmek ne kadar sürer?
Is this seat taken?	Bu yerin sahibi var mı?
May I sit here?	Burada oturabilir miyim?
Would you be good enough to show me around?	Beni gezdirmek lütfünde bulunur musunuz?
Can one go on foot?	Yaya gidilebilir mi?
Can I hire a carriage?	Bir araba tutabilir miyim?
Can one hire a donkey?	Eşek kiralanabilir mi?
Is this the right road for . . . ?	. . .'e giden yol bu mu?
What is the name of the street?	Bu sokağın adı ne?
What is the name of this mosque?	Bu caminin adı ne?
What is the name of this church?	Bu kilisenin adı ne?
How far is Saint Sophia?	Ayasofya ne kadar uzak?
How do I go there?	Oraya nasıl gidilir?
Should one take the bus?	Otobüse mi binmeli?
Is it near?	Yakın mı?
Which way?	Ne taraftan?
This way.	Bu taraftan.
That way.	O taraftan.
Turn left.	Sola dönünüz.
Turn right.	Sağa dönünüz.
Go straight on.	Düz gidiniz.
Take the first road on the right.	Sağdan birinci yola sapınız.
Take the third road on the left.	Soldan üçüncü yola sapınız.
Is there a bus stop near here?	Civarda bir otobüs durağı var mı?
What is this building?	Bu bina ne?
Where can one have a panoramic view of the city?	Şehrin panoramik manzarası nereden görülebilir?
Where is the museum?	Müze nerede?
How much is the admission?	Girişi kaça?
Is it open?	Açık mı?
I was looking for . . . and I took the wrong road.	. . .'e gidecektim, ama yanlış yola sapmışım.
I am lost!	Yolumu kaybettim!
I should like to cross the Bosphorus Bridge.	Boğaziçi köprüsünden geçmek istiyorum.

KEY TO PRONUNCIATION

c (jar), ç (church), g (gale), ğ (lengthen the preceding vowel), h (hill), ı (Cyril), j (Fr. *jeune*), ö (Fr. *peu* or Ger. *Köln*), s (sister), ş (shoe), ü (Fr. *dune* or Ger. *Glück*)

Sightseeing

Go straight till you get to the park.	Parka çıkıncıya kadar düz yürüyünüz.
Can we go in the Topkapı Palace?	Topkapı Sarayına girebilir miyiz?
Is admission free on Sundays?	Pazar günü giriş serbest mi?
Is there a reduction for students?	Öğrenciler için tenzilat var mı?
Where do I leave my camera?	Fotograf makinemi nereye bırakacağım?
May I take photographs in the museum?	Müzede resim çekebilir miyim?
Have you any postcards of the treasures?	Müzedeki eşyanın kartpostalı var mı?
Have you a map of the museum?	Müzenin planı var mı?
Where can I buy a catalogue?	Katalog nerede satılıyor?
Does the street go to the Covered Bazaar?	Bu yol Kapalı Çarşıya gider mi?
We want to go to a Turkish bath.	Bir Türk Hamamına gitmek istiyoruz!
We should like to see the Turkish folk-dancers!	Türk halkoyunlarını seyretmek istiyoruz!
Where can one see belly-dancers?	Göbek oyunu nerede seyredilebilir?
How does one go to the Rumeli Hisar fortress?	Rumeli Hisarına nasıl gidilir?
Have you got a city plan of Istanbul?	Istanbul şehir planı var mı?
How long does it take to cross the Bosphorus?	Boğaziçini geçmek ne kadar sürer?
Is it only fifteen minutes to get from Europe to Asia?	Avrupadan Asyaya geçmek sadece bir çeyrek mi sürer?
How frequent are the ferries?	Araba vapuru sık işler mi?
Is there a non-stop shuttle service?	Gece gündüz aralıksız işliyen bir servis var mı?

KEY TO PRONUNCIATION

c (jar), ç (church), g (gale), ğ (lengthen the preceding vowel), h (hill), ı (Cyril), j (Fr. *jeune*), ö (Fr. *peu* or Ger. *Köln*), s (sister), ş (shoe), ü (Fr. *dune* or Ger. *Glück*)

17 Animals and vegetation

In Turkey one can see three distinct natural vegetation regions. These are the Mediterranean, the Black Sea region and the Continental Anatolia. The Mediterranean region which includes South, West and North-west Turkey is covered with typical maqui at and near sea level, and is followed by a deciduous forest zone at an altitude of 700 metres to 1,200 metres, this later changing to a coniferous forest zone up to more than 2,000 metres. With its great variety of flowers, the Black Sea region is the most densely wooded and the richest forest region of Turkey. It has deciduous humid sub-tropical forest and evergreen bushes up to 800 metres, mixed humid forest between 800-1,500 metres and coniferous forest up to 2,000 metres. Continental Anatolia, on the other hand, is mainly a steppe region, natural forests beginning at an altitude of 1,400 metres, and the upper timber line rising up to 2,800 metres. Forests of these high altitudes are usually composed of coniferous trees which resist extremely low winter temperatures.

Turkey has quite a number of rivers and lakes. Rivers are mainly fed by either rain or melted snow and ice. This causes irregularity and poor navigation. Some Turkish lakes are crater lakes while others are of glacial origin. Most of them are grouped in Eastern and Central Anatolia. The largest lake in Turkey is the Van Gölü which is 3,764 square kilometres and is 1,720 metres above sea level. The lakes of Beyşehir (651 km.^{2}) and Eğirdir (517 km.^{2}) are the largest fresh-water lakes of the group in the Turkish lake district and offer beautiful scenery, crowned with snow-capped mountains, as well as opportunity for fishing and sailing.

On the grazing lands of the Turkish plateau, sheep and cattle are raised in abundance. Oxen, horses, mules and water-buffaloes are numerous. Camels and donkeys are quite popular, but the animal of Turkey is the Ankara goat, which is famous for its transparent, white, lustrous fleece, called mohair. Ankara and Van cats are also world famous. The Ankara cat has long, glossy white fur and eyes of different colours – one blue, one pea-green or amber. It has the reputation of being timid and ill-natured, of not living long and turning deaf and blind toward the end of its life. Van cats are also called swimming cats. They are usually white and ginger in colour.

Over fifteen per cent of cultivated areas in Turkey are devoted to cereals. Wheat, grown on the central plateau, accounts for half the total grain production and is an important export. Other cereals are barley, corn, rye, millet and oats. Turkish sultanas, raisins, figs, pistachios, hazelnuts, almonds, olives, olive oil and attar of roses are other major agricultural products of Turkey, well known in international markets for their fine quality.

Among other agricultural products supplying the home food markets are fresh fruit and vegetables, tea and cheeses.

Animals – Vocabulary

bee	arı	horse	at
bird	kuş	insect	böcek
bull	boğa	lamb	kuzu
butterfly	kelebek	lizard	kertenkele
camel	deve	mosquito	sivrisinek
cat	kedi	mouse	fare
centipede	kırkayak	mule	katır
chicken	piliç	owl	baykuş
cockroach	hamam böceği	ox	öküz
cow	inek	pig	domuz
dog	köpek	rat	sıçan
donkey	eşek	scorpion	akrep
fire-fly	ateş böceği	sheep	koyun
fish	balık	snake	yılan
fly	sinek	stork	leylek
frog	kurbağa	tortoise	kaplumbağa
goat	keçi	wasp	eşek arısı
goose	kaz	water-buffalo	manda
hen	tavuk	wolf	kurt

KEY TO PRONUNCIATION

c (jar), ç (church), a (gale), ğ (lengthen the preceding vowel), h (hill), ı (Cyril), j (Fr. *jeune*), ö (Fr. *peu* or Ger. *Köln*), s (sister), ş (shoe), ü (Fr. *dune* or Ger. Glück)

Vegetation – Vocabulary

apple	elma	orange	portakal
barley	arpa	pear	armut
branch	dal	pine	çam
bush	çalı	pistachios	şam fıstığı
carnation	karanfil	plane	çınar ağacı
cherry	kiraz	plant	bitki
cotton	pamuk	pomegranate	nar
chestnut	kestane	poplar	kavak
corn	mısır	quince	ayva
cypress	selvi	rice	pirinç
flower	çiçek	root	kök
fig	incir	rose	gül
forest	orman	rye	çavdar
fruit	meyva	strawberry	çilek
grape	üzüm	tangerine	mandalina
grapefruit	greyfurt	tobacco	tütün
grass	çimen	tree	ağaç
hazelnuts	fındık	trunk	gövde
leaf	yaprak	tulip	lâle
lemon	limon	vine	bağ
melon	kavun	wheat	buğday
oak	meşe	walnut	ceviz
olive	zeytin	water-melon	karpuz
opium	afyon	wood	koru

Phrases

Are there mosquitoes?	Sivrisinek var mı?
What was that, a scorpion or a a centipede?	O neydi, akrep mi, kırkayak mı?
They are only cockroaches.	Onlar sadece hamamböcekleri.
This slope is very rocky.	Bu yamaç çok kayalık.
The grass is very dry.	Otlar çok kurumuş.
It is dangerous to light a fire.	Ateş yakmak çok tehlikeli.

KEY TO PRONUNCIATION

c (jar), ç (church), g (gale), ğ (lengthen the preceding vowel), h (hill), ı (Cyril), j (Fr. *jeune*), ö (Fr. *peu* or Ger. *Köln*), s (sister), ş (shoe), ü (Fr. *dune* or Ger. Glück)

Animals and vegetations

There is a lot of dust.	Çok toz var.
Are there many snakes around?	Etrafta çok yılan var mı?
I like riding a donkey.	Eşeğe binmesini severim.
One can see storks on all chimney tops in southern Turkey.	İnsan Türkyenin güneyinde her baca üstünde bir leylek görebilir.
What trees are they?	Bunlar ne ağaçları?
These pale green leaved trees are olive trees.	Bu soluk yeşil yapraklı ağaçlar zeytin ağaçlarıdır.
What do you call these flowers?	Bu çiçeklerin adı nedir?
They are tulips and carnations.	Onlar lâle ve karanfildir.
Is this a melon field?	Bu kavun tarlası mı?
Is this an orange orchard?	Bu bir portakal bahçesi mi?
Turkish hazel-nuts and tobacco are world-famous.	Türk fındık ve tütünleri dünyaca tanınmıştır.
Is this a barley or a rye field?	Bu arpa tarlası mı yoksa çavdar tarlası mı?
Bursa is famous for its chestnut trees.	Bursa kestane ağaçlariyle tanınmıştır.
Does tea grow in Turkey?	Türkiyede çay yetişir mi?
Yes, it grows in the Rize region.	Evet, Rize bölgesinde yetişir.

KEY TO PRONUNCIATION

c (jar), ç (church), g (gale), ğ (lengthen the preceding vowel), h (hill), ı (Cyril), j (Fr. *jeune*), ö (Fr. *peu* or Ger. *Köln*), s (sister), ş (shoe), ü (Fr. *dune* or Ger. *Glück*)

18 Hunting and fishing

Turkey is a land rich in fish and game, both in variety and in abundance. However, as there is danger of extinction of various birds and animals, hunting has been restricted to the shooting of only wild boars and mountain goats.

Hunters from abroad are expected to come to Turkey in groups of five or more, having had their hunting licences duly certified by the Turkish General Consulate or the Turkish Tourism and Information Office in their country. This licence together with the hunter's identification card has to be forwarded to the Travel Agent or the Tour Operator in charge of the group in Turkey three weeks prior to the group's departure so that the Agent can obtain a valid licence for hunting from the authorities concerned. Once he has obtained the permission he will inform the hunting party in England thus enabling them to import their hunting rifles and cartridges into Turkey.

It would be advisable to contact the Turkish Tourism and Information Office in your area for up-to-date details and for the beginning and end of the hunting season which varies from year to year.

There is no requirement for a fishing licence in Turkey.

Vocabulary

animal	hayvan	duck	ördek
badger	porsuk	fish	balık
bass	levrek	fish, to	balık tutmak
bear	ayı	fishing	balıkçılık
boar	erkek domuz	fox	tilki
brown bear	kahverengi ayı	geese	kazlar
carp	sazan balığı	goose	kaz
cat	kedi	goat	keçi
deer	geyik	hook	olta kancası
dove	kumru	hunt, to	avlamak

KEY TO PRONUNCIATION

c (jar), ç (church), g (gale), ğ (lengthen the preceding vowel), h (hill), ı (Cyril), j (Fr. *jeune*), ö (Fr. *peu* or Ger. *Köln*), s (sister), ş (shoe), ü (Fr. *dune* or Ger. Glück)

Hunting and fishing

hunting	avcılık	ram	koç
hunting club	avcılık kulübü	shoot, to	tüfekle vurmak
line	olta	shooting	tüfekle vuruş
lion	aslan	squirrel	sincap
lynx	vaşak	stork	leylek
mallard	yaban ördeği	tackle	balık tutma takımı
owl	baykuş		
panther	panter	teal	çamurca ördeği (nehir ördeği)
partridge	keklik		
pheasant	sülün	tiger	kaplan
pigeon	güvercin	trout	alabalık
pike	turna balığı	wild	yaban
pintail	çil (keklik) (göl ördeği)	wild boar	yaban domuzu
		wild duck	yaban ördeği
porcupine	kirpi	wild goat	yaban keçisi
quail	bıldırcın	wolf	kurt
rabbit	tavşan		

Phrases

I want to join a hunt.	Ava çıkmak istiyorum.
I want to become a member of a hunting club.	Avcılık Kulübüne üye olmak istiyorum.
What is the address of the hunting club?	Avcılık Kulübünün adresi nedir?
How do I apply for a hunting licence?	Av tezkeresi almak için nasıl başvurmam gerek?
Do they want my photographs?	Fotograf gerekli mi?
Has your local hunting licence been certified by the Turkish General Consulate?	Av tezkereniz Türkiye Başkonsolosluğunca tasdik edildi mi?
I have shown it to the Turkish Tourism and Information Office and they have certified it.	Türkiye Turizm ve Haberler Bürosuna gösterdim ve onlar tasdik ettiler.

KEY TO PRONUNCIATION

c (jar), ç (church), g (gale), ğ (lengthen the preceding vowel), h (hill), ı (Cyril), j (Fr. *jeune*), ö (Fr. *peu* or Ger. *Köln*), s (sister), ş (shoe), ü (Fr. *dune* or Ger. Glück)

Hunting and fishing

Is there any restriction on the amount of cartridges that I can take with me?	Beraberimde götüreceğim fişek miktarı kısıtlanmış mıdır?
Yes, you should ask the authorities concerned before purchasing any.	Evet, satın almadan önce ilgili makamlara sormalısınız!
Is there a charge for the hunting licence?	Av tezkeresi için bir şey ödemek gerek mi?
Yes, there is a charge but the Tour Operator pays it on your behalf.	Evet, var ama Seyahat Acentası sizin adınıza bunu ödüyor.
Does he provide me with a hunting dog?	Bana bir av köpeği de sağlıyor mu?
Yes, he pays not only for the hunting dog but for beaters as well.	Sadece köpek sağlamakla kalmıyor ayrıca kışkırtıcıları da temin ediyor.
Does one need a fishing licence?	Balık tutmak için bir tezkere almak lazım mı?
No. No fishing licence is required.	Hayır. Balık tutmak için tezkereye lüzum yok.
Is there a bag limit?	Tutulacak balık adedi sınırlandırılmış mıdır?
No, there is no bag limit.	Hayır, böyle bir tahdit yok.

KEY TO PRONUNCIATION

c (jar), ç (church), g (gale), ğ (lengthen the preceding vowel), h (hill), ı (Cyril), (Fr. *jeune*), ö (Fr. *peu* or Ger. *Köln*), s (sister), ş (shoe), ü (Fr. *dune* or Ger. Glück)

19   Accident and loss of property

Vocabulary

accident	kaza	insurance policy	sigorta poliçesi
ambulance	cankurtaran	jewellery	mücevherler
artificial respiration	suni teneffüs	knocked down	yere serilmiş
bracelet	bilezik	lorry	kamyon
briefcase	evrak çantası	lose, to	kaybetmek
broken	kırık	lost	kaybolmuş
camera	fotoğraf makinesi	luggage	bagaj, yol eşyası
certificate	rapor, belge	money	para
collide, to	çarpışmak	passport	pasaport
complaint	şikâyet	police	polis
consciousness	şuur, bilinç	purse	para çantası, kese
damage	zarar	reward	mükâfat
dangerous	tehlikeli	ring	yüzük
diamond	pırlanta, elmas	stolen	çalınmış
first aid outfit	ilkyardım malzemesi (cihazı)	stretcher	sedye
		tow, to	çekmek
gloves	eldivenler	travellers' cheques	travelers çek
handbag	elçantası (para çantası)	umbrella	şemsiye
hospital	hastane	watch	saat, kolsaati
injured	yaralanmış	witness	tanık, şahit
insurance company	sigorta şirketi	wound	yara

KEY TO PRONUNCIATION

c (jar), ç (church), g (gale), ğ (lengthen the preceding vowel), h (hill), ı (Cyril), j (Fr. *jeune*), ö (Fr. *peu* or Ger. *Köln*), s (sister), ş (shoe), ü (Fr. *dune* or Ger. Glück)

Phrases

Help! Help!	İmdat! İmdat!
Call an ambulance!	Bir cankurtaran çağırın!
A man is dying!	Bir adam ölüyor!
There has been an accident.	Bir kaza oldu.
The car and the lorry collided.	Otomobille kamyon çarpıştı.
He has been knocked down.	O yere devrildi (serildi).
Please call the police.	Lütfen polisi çağrın.
Where is the nearest police station?	En yakın polis karakolu nerde?
Please phone at once for an ambulance!	Lütfen cankurtaran arabası için telefon ediniz!
Will you please call a doctor quickly!	Çabuk bir doktor çağırınız lütfen!
An accident has just occurred at ...	... da şimdi bir kaza oldu.
There are people seriously injured.	Ağır yaralı insan var.
He must not be moved. It is very dangerous.	Yerinden oynatılmamalı. Çok tehlikeli.
No one is seriously injured.	Ağır yaralı kimse yok.
There is some damage.	Zarar var. (Hasar var).
Will you kindly act as witness?	Tanıklık (şahitlik) etmek lütfünde bulunur musunuz?
Did you see the accident?	Kazayı gördünüz mü?
May I ask your name and address?	Adınızı ve adresinizi öğrenebilir miyim?
Don't touch anything until the police arrive.	Polis gelinceye kadar hiç bir şeye dokunmayınız!
Please move aside!	Lütfen kenara çekilin!
Place the injured person on a stretcher.	Yaralıyı sedyeye yatırınız.
Where is the hospital?	Hastane nerede?
Are you injured?	Yaralı mısınız?
I am not injured.	Ben yaralı değilim.

KEY TO PRONUNCIATION

c (jar), ç (church), g (gale), ğ (lengthen the preceding vowel), h (hill), ı (Cyril), j (Fr. *jeune*), ö (Fr. *peu* or Ger. *Köln*), s (sister), ş (shoe), ü (Fr. *dune* or Ger. *Glück*)

Accident and loss of property

My friend is in bad shape.	Arkadaşımın hali fena.
Can I help you?	Size yardım edebilir miyim?
Have you a first-aid outfit?	İlkyardım çantanız var mı?
Here is my insurance policy.	İşte sigorta poliçem.
Apply to the insurance company.	Sigorta Şirketine başvurunuz.
Please give me a copy of the police report.	Polis raporunun (zabtının) bir kopyesini lütfen veriniz.
Please get a garage to take the car away.	Otomobili çekip götürmek üzere lütfen bir garaja haber veriniz.
My car has broken down ... km. from here, on the road.	Buradan ... km. mesafede otomobilim bozuldu, yol üstünde.
Can you have it towed here?	Buraya çektirtebilir misiniz?
He has lost consciousness.	Şuurunu kaybetti. (kendini kaybetti.)
Can you help me to carry him?	Onu taşımama yardım edebilir misiniz?
Can you dress this wound?	Bu yarayı sarabilir misiniz?
He needs artificial respiration.	Suni teneffüse ihtiyacı var.
I have lost ...	... ı kaybettim.
I have forgotten ...	... ı unuttum.
My ... has been stolen.	Benim ... ı çaldılar.
— passport	— pasaportumu
— purse	— para çantamı
— money	— paramı
— jewellery	— mücevherlerimi
— camera	— fotograf makinemi
— briefcase	— evrak çantamı
— watch	— kol saatimi
— car documents	— otomobil belgelerimi
— luggage	— eşyalarımı
— umbrella	— şemsiyemi
— gloves	— eldivenlerimi
— insurance policy	— sigorta poliçemi
I wish to make a complaint.	Bir şikâyette bulunmak istiyorum
I have a complaint.	Bir şikâyetim var.

KEY TO PRONUNCIATION

c (jar), ç (church), g (gale), ğ (lengthen the preceding vowel), h (hill), ı (Cyril), j (Fr. *jeune*), ö (Fr. *peu* or Ger. *Köln*), s (sister), ş (shoe), ü (Fr. *dune* or Ger. Glück)

Please give me a certificate.	Lütfen bana bir rapor (belge) veriniz.
I am offering a reward.	Bulana mükâfat vereceğim.
I am leaving you my address.	Size adresimi bırakıyorum.

KEY TO PRONUNCIATION

c (jar), ç (church), g (gale), ğ (lengthen the preceding vowel), h (hill), ı (Cyril), j (Fr. *jeune*), ö (Fr. *peu* or Ger. *Köln*), s (sister), ş (shoe), ü (Fr. *dune* or Ger. Glück)

20 Visiting the doctor

Illness

abscess	abse, çıban	cramp	kramp, adele tutulması
ache	ağrı		
allergic to	alerjisi olmak	cure	ilâç, kür
appendicitis	apandisit	cure, to	tedavi etmek, iyi etmek
asthma	astım, nefes darlığı		
		cut	kesme, kesiş
bandage	bandaj, sargı	dentist	dişçi
bite	ısırık	diabetes	şeker hastalığı, diabet
blister	kabarcık, uçuk		
boil	çıban	diarrhoea	amel, ishal, diyare
bruise	bere, çürük		
breath	nefes	diet	perhiz
burn	yanık	diphtheria	difteri, kuş palazı
cancer	kanser		
chicken-pox	suçiçeği	dizziness	baş dönmesi
chill	soğuk alma, üşütme	doctor	doktor
		epidemic	salgın
cold	nezle	epilepsy	sara hastalığı
constipation	kabızlık	faint	baygınlık, bayılma
consultation	konsültasyon, istişare		
		faint, to	bayılmak
convalescence	nekahet	fever	ateş
convulsions	titremeler	filling	dolgu
corn	nasır	first aid	ilkyardım
cough	öksürük	fracture	kırık

KEY TO PRONUNCIATION

c (jar), ç (church), g (gale), ğ (lengthen the preceding vowel), h (hill), ı (Cyril), j (Fr. *jeune*), ö (Fr. *peu* or Ger. *Köln*), s (sister), ş (shoe), ü (Fr. *dune* or Ger. *Glück*)

Visiting the doctor

hay-fever	saman nezlesi	small-pox	çiçek
headache	başağrısı	scarlatina	kızıl
health	sağlık	splint	kıymık, kırık
hiccups	hıçkırık		kemik sarmağa
hospital	hastane		mahsus tahta
illness	hastalık	spot	benek, leke, nokta
indigestion	hazımsızlık	sprain	mafsal burkulması
influenza	grip, salgın nezle	sting	arı sokması, diken
injection	enjeksiyon, iğne		batması
insomnia	uykusuzluk	stitch	dikiş, sırtta
itch	kaşıntı		duyulan ani acı
jaundice	sarılık	stomach-ache	karın ağrısı
measles	kızamık	sty	arpacık
mumps	kabakulak	sunstroke	güneş çarpması
nausea	bulantı	sunburn	güneş yanığı
nurse	hastabakıcı	surgeon	cerrah, operatör
operation	ameliyat	surgery	ameliyat odası
pain	acı, sızı, ağrı	swallowing	yutma
patient	hasta	swelling	şişme
poison	zehir	swell, to	şişmek, kabarmak
pneumonia	zatürre, akciğer	temperature	ısı, hararet
	iltihabı	toothache	diş ağrısı
pleurisy	zatülcenp, göğüs	treatment	tedavi
	zarı iltihabı	typhoid fever	tifo
prescription	reçete	typhus fever	tifüs
remedy	ilâç, deva	vomit	kusma
rheumatism	romatizma	whooping	boğmaca
scar	yara izi	cough	
scarlet fever	kızıl	wound	yara
scratch	kaşıma, tırmalama	X-ray	Rontgen
sick	hasta	yellow fever	sarı humma
sea-sickness	deniz tutması		

Parts of the body

abdomen	karın	arm	kol
ankle	ayak bileği	armpit	koltuk altı

KEY TO PRONUNCIATION

c (jar), ç (church), g (gale), ğ (lengthen the preceding vowel), h (hill), ı (Cyril), j (Fr. *jeune*), ö (Fr. *peu* or Ger. *Köln*), s (sister), ş (shoe), ü (Fr. *dune* or Ger. *Glück*)

back	sırt, arka	joint	mafsal
backbone	omurga, belkemiği	kidney	böbrek
bladder	idrar torbası	knee	diz
blood	kan	knee-cap	diz kapağı
body	vücut	leg	bacak
bone	kemik	lip	dudak
bowels	barsaklar	liver	karaciğer
calf	baldır	lung	akciğer
cheek	yanak	mouth	ağız
chest	göğüs	muscle	adele
chin	çene	neck	boyun
ear	kulak	nose	burun
elbow	dirsek	nostril	burun deliği
eye	göz	pelvis	kalça kemiği ovası
eyelid	gözkapağı		boşluğu, leğen
face	yüz	rib	kaburga kemiği
false teeth	takma diş	shoulder	omuz
finger	parmak	skin	deri
finger-nail	tırnak	skull	kafatası
foot	ayak	sole	taban
forehead	alın	stomach	mide
gall bladder	safra kesesi	temple	şakak
gum	dişeti	throat	boğaz
hair	saç	thigh	uyluk, but
hairs	kıllar	thumb	başparmak
hand	el	toe	ayak parmağı
head	baş	tongue	dil
heart	kalp	tonsil	bademcik
heel	topuk	tooth	diş
hip	kalça, kaba et	vein	damar
intestine	barsak	waist	bel
jaw	çene kemiği	wrist	bilek

Questions asked by the doctor

Write your name and address.   Adınızı ve adresinizi yazınız.
How old are you?   Kaç yaşındasınız?

KEY TO PRONUNCIATION

c (jar), ç (church), g (gale), ğ (lengthen the preceding vowel), h (hill), ı (Cyril), j (Fr. *jeune*), ö (Fr. *peu* or Ger. *Köln*), s (sister), ş (shoe), ü (Fr. *dune* or Ger. *Glück*)

Visiting the doctor

Have you a sickness insurance?	Hastalık sigortanız var mı?
How long have you been ill?	Ne zamandanberi hastasınız?
Undress, lie down.	Soyununuz, sırtüstü yatınız.
Breathe quietly.	Nefes alınız.
What illnesses have you had?	Ne hastalıklar geçirdiniz?
What have you eaten and drunk?	Ne yediniz ve ne içtiniz?
What medicine have you taken?	Ne ilâç aldınız?
I am going to have your ... tested.	... i muayene ettireceğim.
I am going to give you a hypodermic injection.	Deri altına bir enjeksiyon yapacağım.
You will take ... per day.	Günde ... alacaksınız.
— tablets	— tablet
— pastilles	— pastil
— drops	— damla
You must not eat ...	... yememelisiniz.
You must not exert yourself!	Kendinizi yormamalısınız!
Rub yourself with ...	Vücudunuzu ... la oğuşturunuz.
You must stay in bed for ... days.	... gün için yatakta yatmalısınız.
You must go to hospital.	Hastaneye gitmelisiniz.
You must have an operation.	Ameliyat olmalısınız.
Have you any family?	Aileniz var mı?
Give this prescription to the chemist.	Bu reçeteyi eczacıya veriniz.
Come back and see me again.	Tekrar gelip beni görünüz.

Complaints of the patient

I have a pain here,	Burası ağrıyor
— when coughing.	— öksürürken.
— when breathing.	— nefes alırken.
— when swallowing.	— yutkunurken.
I have a headache.	Başım ağrıyor.
I have a fever.	Ateşim var.
My child is ill.	Çocuğum hasta.

KEY TO PRONUNCIATION

c (jar), ç (church), g (gale), ğ (lengthen the preceding vowel), h (hill), ı (Cyril), j (Fr. *jeune*), ö (Fr. *peu* or Ger. *Köln*), s (sister), ş (shoe), ü (Fr. *dune* or Ger. Glück)

Visiting the doctor 151

I have diarrhoea.	Amel oldum.
I have no appetite.	İştiham yok.
I have a chill.	Soğuk aldım.
I feel dizzy.	Başım dönüyor.
I feel very breathless.	Nefesim daralıyor.
I feel sick.	İçim bulanıyor.
I have pains all over.	Her tarafım ağrıyor.
My stomach is upset.	Midem bozulmuş.
I have a cough.	Öksürük oldum.
I am spitting blood.	Kan tükürüyorum.
I have blood in my urine.	İdrarımda kan var.
I fainted.	Bayıldım. (Baygınlık geçirdim.)
I am pregnant.	Hamileyim. (Gebeyim.)
I have lost blood.	Kan kaybettim.
I have heart trouble.	Kalp hastalığım var. (Kalbimde bozukluk, bir ağrı var.)
I fell down.	Düşüp yuvarlandım.
I have had a shock.	Bir şok geçirdim.
I have been stung by an insect.	Beni bir böcek soktu.
I have sprained my wrist.	Bileğimi incittim.
I have something in my eye.	Gözüme bir şey kaçtı.
I have been vaccinated against ...	... a karşı aşım var.
I am allergic to ...	... a karşı alerjim var.
My dressing is hurting me.	Sargım acıtıyor.
I feel worse.	Kendimi daha fena hissediyorum.
I feel better.	Kendimi daha iyi hissediyorum.
Tea-spoons.	Çay kaşığı.
Table-spoons.	Yemek kaşığı.
Before, after meals.	Yemeklerden önce, sonra.
During meals.	Yemek arasında.

At the Doctor's

I must see a doctor!	Doktora gitmeliyim!
I want to make an appointment for ...	... için bir randevu reca ediyorum.

KEY TO PRONUNCIATION

c (jar), ç (church), g (gale), ğ (lengthen the preceding vowel), h (hill), ı (Cyril), j (Fr. *jeune*), ö (Fr. *peu* or Ger. *Köln*), s (sister), ş (shoe), ü (Fr. *dune* or Ger. *Glück*)

Visiting the doctor

Take me to a doctor!	Beni bir doktora götürünüz!
Please take me to a hospital!	Lütfen beni hastaneye götürünüz!
I want a complete check-up.	Çekap yaptırmak istiyorum.
I want to have my lungs X-rayed.	Ciğerlerimin rontgenini çektirmek istiyorum.
I have something in my ear.	Kulağımda bir şey var.
I cannot hear well.	İyi duyamıyorum.
I have a sore throat.	Boğazım batıyor.
My tonsils are swollen.	Bademciklerim şişmiş.
My pulse is very irregular.	Nabzım düzgün atmıyor.
I need a pair of spectacles.	Gözlüğe ihtiyacım var.
I have sprained my ankle.	Ayak bileğimi incittim.
I am suffering from an ulcer.	Ülserden muztaribim.
Please take my temperature.	Lütfen hararetime bakınız. (Lütfen derecemi alınız.)
Will you give me a prescription?	Bir reçete verir misiniz?
Should I stay in bed?	Yatakta yatmam lazım mı?
Where can I have this prescription prepared?	Bu reçeteyi nerede yaptırtabilirim?
What are your surgery hours?	Muayene saatleriniz nedir?
What is your charge, Doctor?	Viziteniz ne kadar, doktor?
You must be moved to hospital.	Hastaneye kaldırılmanız lazım.
I think your leg is broken.	Galiba ayağınız kırılmış.
Has a taxi knocked you down?	Size bir taksi mi çarptı?
Let me help you to walk.	Yürümcnize yardım edeyim.
Would you please dress this wound?	Lütfen bu yarayı sarabilir misiniz?
The patient must not be disturbed!	Hasta rahatsız edilmemeli!

At the Dentist's

I must see a dentist!	Bir dişçiye gitmeliyim!
Can you recommend me a good dentist?	Bana iyi bir diş doktoru tavisye edebilir misiniz?
Please come into the surgery.	Muayene odasına buyrun.

KEY TO PRONUNCIATION

c (jar), ç (church), g (gale), ğ (lengthen the preceding vowel), h (hill), ı (Cyril), j (Fr. *jeune*), ö (Fr. *peu* or Ger. *Köln*), s (sister), ş (shoe), ü (Fr. *dune* or Ger. Glück)

Visiting the doctor

Let me see your teeth.	Dişlerinize bakayım.
Which one aches?	Hangisi ağrıyor?
This one, at the back.	Buradaki, şu arkadaki diş.
The root is decayed.	Kökü çürümüş.
Please remove the gold crown.	Altın kronu çıkarınız.
The tooth must be extracted.	Dişin çıkarılması lazım.
I have lost a filling.	Dolgum düştü.
Will you please fill it?	Lütfen doldurur musunuz?
Is it worth saving this tooth?	Bu dişi kurtarmağa değer mi?
I want to have it taken out.	Bunu çıkarmanızı istiyorum.
Open your mouth, please!	Lütfen, ağzınızı açınız!
Rinse with a little water.	Bir parça suyla çalkalayınız.
Close your mouth now.	Şimdi ağzınızı kapayınız.
This time open your mouth wider.	Bu sefer ağzınızı daha fazla açınız.
Do not close it until I tell you.	Ben söylemeden kapatmayınız.
Does that hurt?	Acıtıyor mu?
You are hurting me!	Acıtıyorsunuz!
Will you give me an anaesthetic?	Anastezi yapacak mısınız?
My gums are swollen.	Dişetlerim şişmiş.
The nerve is exposed.	Siniri açıkta.
I feel both cold and hot.	Hem soğuğu, hem sıcağı hissediyorum.
There is a constant bleeding.	Devamlı bir kanama var.
Will you do something for the time being?	Şimdilik bir şey yapabilir misiniz?
Please give me something to stop the ache.	Lütfen ağrıyı durdutacak bir şey veriniz.
Don't eat for at least three hours.	En az üç saat bir şey yemeyiniz.
What are your fees?	Viziteniz ne kadar?

KEY TO PRONUNCIATION

c (jar), ç (church), g (gale), ğ (lengthen the preceding vowel), h (hill), ı (Cyril), j (Fr. *jeune*), ö (Fr. *peu* or Ger. *Köln*), s (sister), ş (shoe), ü (Fr. *dune* or Ger. *Glück*)

21　　　　　　　　　　Calendar of events in Turkey

January

New Year's Day
Ski Competitions in Bursa,
Kayseri, Ankara, Erzurum, etc.

February

Folk Dance Festival.

March

Celebrations commemorating the
Anniversary of the Gallipoli
Victory, 18 March.

April

Uludağ Winter Festival.
National Sovereignty and
Children's Day, 23 April. (Holiday)
Spring Festival of Manisa,
15–23 April.
Tulip Festival of Istanbul,
23 April.

May

Youth Day, 19 May. (Holiday)
Festival of Ephesus.
Festival of Pergamum.
Festival of Antalya.
Art and Culture Festival of
Yunus Emre.

Ocak

Yılbaşı Tatili
Kayak Yarışmaları Bursa,
Kayseri, Ankara, Erzurum.

Şubat

Halkoyunları Festivali.

Mart

Çanakkale Zaferi şenlikleri,
18 Mart.

Nisan

Uludağ Kış Festivali.
Milli Egemenlik ve Çocuk
Günü, 23 Nisan. (Tatil)
Manisa Mesir Festivali,
15–23 Nisan.
Istanbul Lâle Festivali, 23 Nisan.

Mayıs

Gençlik Bayramı, 19 Mayıs. (Tatil)
Efes Festivali.
Bergama Festivali.
Antalya Festivali.
Yunus Emre Festivali.

KEY TO PRONUNCIATION

c (jar), ç (church), g (gale), ğ (lengthen the preceding vowel), h (hill), ı (Cyril), j (Fr. *jeune*), ö (Fr. *peu* or Ger. *Köln*), s (sister), ş (shoe), ü (Fr. *dune* or Ger. *Glück*)

June

Istanbul Art and Culture Festival.
Anniversay of the Proclamation
of Turkish as the official language.
Karaman.
Amasya Atatürk's Day.
Wrestling Games of Kırkpınar.
St. Peter's Day – Antioch,
29 June.

July

Navy Day (Sea Contests), 1 July.
Istanbul, İzmir, Trabzon, etc.
Nasreddin Hoca Festival, Akşehir,
5–10 July.
Sword and Shield Festival of
Bursa, 7–12 July.
Festival of Erdek
Amasra Festival, 30 July.
Samsun Fair, 1–31 July.
Bursa Fair, 7–31 July.
Film Festival in Antalya.

August

Feast of Holy Virgin of Ephesus,
15 August.
Gaziantep Festival.
Nevşehir – Commemorative
Ceremonies of Hacı Bektaş Veli,
16 August.
Balıkesir Fair, 6 August –
6 September.
İZMİR INTERNATIONAL
FAIR, 20 August – 20 September.
Victory Day, 30 August. (Holiday)

Haziran

Istanbul Kültür vc Sanat Festivali.
Karaman Türk Dili Bayramı.

Amasya Atatürk Günü.
Kırkpınar Güreşleri.
Antakya Sen Piyer Ayini,
29 Haziran.

Temmuz

Deniz Bayramı, 1 Temmuz
Istanbul, İzmir, Trabzon.
Nasreddin Hoca Festivali, Akşehir,
5–10 Temmuz.
Kılıç Kalkan Festivali Bursa,
7–12 Temmuz.
Erdek Festivali.
Amasra Festivali, 30 Temmuz.
Samsun Fuarı, 1–31 Temmuz.
Bursa Fuarı, 7–31 Temmuz.
Antalya Film Festivali.

Ağustos

Meryemana ayini, 15 Ağustos.

Gaziantep Festivali.
Nevşehir – Hacı Bektaş Veli'yi
Anma Töreni, 16 Ağustos.

Balıkesir Fuarı, 6 Ağustos –
6 Eylül.
İZMİR ENTERNASYONAL
FUARI, 20 Ağustos – 20 Eylül.
Zafer Bayramı, 30 Ağustos. (Tatil)

KEY TO PRONUNCIATION

c (jar), ç (church), g (gale), ğ (lengthen the preceding vowel), h (hill), ı (Cyril),
j (Fr. *jeune*), ö (Fr. *peu* or Ger. *Köln*), s (sister), ş (shoe), ü (Fr. *dune* or Ger.
Glück)

Trojan Horse Festival in Çanakkale.	Çanakkale Truva Festivali.
Victory Festivities of Afyon, 26–30 August.	Afyon Zafer Şenlikleri, 26–30 Ağustos.
Festival of Mersin.	Mersin Gözne Festivali.

September — Eylül

Congress of Sivas Day, 3 September.	Sıvas Kongresi Günü, 3 Eylül.
Festival of Aydın.	Aydın Festivali.
Festival of Cappadocia.	Göreme Festivali.
İzmir Liberation Day, 9 September.	İzmir Kurtuluş Günü, 9 Eylül.
Festival of Aphrodisias, 15–17 September.	Afrodisyas Festivali, 15–17 Eylül.
Festival of Pamukkale.	Pamukkale Festivali.
Festival of Iznik (Nicaea).	Iznik Festivali.
Kayseri Fair, 25 September–15 October.	Kayseri Fuarı, 25 Eylül–15 Ekim.

October — Ekim

Festival of Trabzon, 25 October.	Trabzon Fetih Şenlikleri, 25 Ekim.
Antalya Fair, 1–10 October.	Antalya Fuarı, 1–10 Ekim.
Mersin Fair, 20 October – 20 November.	Mersin Fuarı, 20 Ekim–20 Kasım.
ANNIVERSARY OF THE TURKISH REPUBLIC, 29 October. (Holiday)	CUMHURIYET BAYRAMI, 29 Ekim. (Tatil)

December — Aralık.

Festival of Mevlana Commemorative ceremonies of Mevlana Celaleddin Rumi, Founder of the Whirling Dervishes.	Mevlana ihtifali.
St. Nicholas Festival.	Noel Baba Festivali.

KEY TO PRONUNCIATION

c (jar), ç (church), (gale), ğ (lengthen the preceding vowel), h (hill), ı (Cyril), j (Fr. *jeune*), ö (Fr. *peu* or Ger. *Köln*), s (sister), ş (shoe), ü (Fr. *dune* or Ger. *Glück*)